The Lord's Prayer for Entrepreneurs

Unlock Success and Build God's Kingdom Through Your Business

by Derek Tye

Derek Tye
2-19-21

The Lord's Prayer for Entrepreneurs
© 2019 by Derek Tye
www.DerekTye.com

This title is also available in Kindle format.
Companion workbook available at
www.kingdombusinessbreakthrough.com/workbook

Published by 100X Publishing
Vacaville, CA
www.100Xacademy.com

Front cover design by Daniel Atkins.

ISBN: 978-1-6894-5088-1

Printed in the United States of America

"Derek Tye has written a book that encourages entrepreneurs of faith to follow God to fully achieve success in their business. It gives them the freedom to be successful and influential in their business for God's purposes."
—Amos Johnson Jr, Founder of Church for Entrepreneurs

"Derek has written a book that encourages and equips the entrepreneur who wants to be a Kingdom entrepreneur. He understands that your Kingdom business *is* your ministry. A Kingdom business is not just one that gives some of its profits to ministries. Of course it includes generosity. A Kingdom business is owned by the King and operated under His influence. My favorite parts were his brilliant insight into the Lord's prayer and how it applies to business. Get ready to see the Kingdom in business more clearly!"
—Jim Baker, Senior Leader of Zion Christian Fellowship, author, Founder of WealthWithGod.com

"In *The Lord's Prayer for Entrepreneurs*, Derek Tye has fashioned a book that speaks to the spirit of Christian entrepreneurship. With the Lord's Prayer as a frame of reference, Derek shares simple, personal and actionable insights that readers can truly take to heart and put to use. Derek's journey is an encouraging reminder that God multiplies our efforts as we co-create with Him to redeem a fallen world."
—Chuck Proudfit, Founder and President, At Work on Purpose

"*The Lord's Prayer for Entrepreneurs* is a magnificent launch pad for anyone who desires to jump into true Kingdom entrepreneurship. Derek's personal and pragmatic approach demystifies one of the Bible's most profound prayers through the eyes and heart of a successful entrepreneur. It's filled with easy-to-implement, practical steps to help you walk out your calling and your marketplace destiny. A keeper!"

—Dr. Jim Harris, author of *Our Unfair Advantage: Unleash the Power of Holy Spirit in Your Business*

"For the new entrepreneur, for the seasoned entrepreneur and for the entrepreneur who is almost ready to give up your dream...this book is for you. In *The Lord's Prayer for Entrepreneurs*, Derek takes you on a journey with him through his long career as an entrepreneur, to pull back the curtain and show you not only his path to success, but also the failures and how he overcame them. His storytelling is so unique, weaving each lesson learned into the framework of the Lord's Prayer in the Bible. He challenges commonly held definitions of "financial success" and "influence." He causes you to examine your motivation for building your business and proposes a revolutionary and powerful way to reframe your purpose. As you apply Derek's framework to your business, you will begin to find more peace and joy in your entrepreneurial journey. What is remarkable to me as a Christian, is how Derek shows us that the Bible is not only a guidebook for life, it is a handbook of successful business practices when you know where to look. Luckily for us, Derek has done all of that legwork in advance. He has pored over biblical stories and teachings, pulling out the precise nuggets of truth that serve as a roadmap to fulfilling our dream as entrepreneurs. As a neuroscientist, I am equally as intrigued by the way the Kingdom principles Derek outlines to become successful in business are also supported by principles of science. For example, when we learn to use business to not further our own agenda, when we look to attain financial success and influence not to build our own egos, but instead to achieve a greater impact on the world, the pressure to "succeed" based on the world's standards of success begins to fade. And, as your stress lowers, a wonderful change begins to happen in your brain...you become more creative. You enter then into the state of mind where million-dollar ideas arise. *The Lord's Prayer for Entrepreneurs* is truly a work of divine inspiration. I am honored and blessed to be among the first to read this masterful book. It will change your business. It will change you. I can't wait to read it again and again."

—Darlene A. Mayo, M.D., Neurosurgeon, Neuroscientist, CEO, AVUCA M.D., PLLC

Table of Contents

Acknowledgments

To God, for whom I exist. All promotion comes from Him. To my wife, Jessica, who makes every day amazing for me and our children. To my children, for giving me another reason to model God's example of fatherhood and inspiring me to be a king in my home taking care of my queen, princes and princesses. Specifically, to Montana Tye, my first-born son who is very entrepreneurial. To Maxwell Tye, my second son who is super smart and challenges me every day. To Parker Tye, my third son who is the sweetest boy I have ever met. To Gabrielle Tye, my first daughter who stole my heart and continues to steal it every day with her smile. To Liliana Tye, my second daughter. She is the most joyful girl you have ever met. To my mom, who has always encouraged me that I could be anything I wanted to be and for showing me Christ in action throughout my life. To my dad, who had strong faith in God and believed in me. To my friend Jimmy Moore, for his advice on writing my first book. To Eric Newberry, for helping me sort out some of the biblical references. And a special thank you to Krista Dunk, my publisher, for her wise insight and coaching to bring this book from a dream into reality!

Purpose

The purpose of this book is to show entrepreneurs that God:

- Loves them,
- Wants them to pursue the unique calling of being a business owner, and
- Wants them to build His Kingdom through this unique vision.

These actions are accomplished only through a strong Kingdom revelation, clarity to see what to do and courage to act this out every day. Specifically, the revelation from this book comes from my interpretation of the Lord's Prayer in context of being a business leader. This book will serve the Kingdom business community by providing God's vision, entrepreneurial purpose, personal stories and practical action steps to walk out our calling. Please note, this book is not an official church study on the topic of faith in business. It represents one entrepreneur's thoughts and prayers. Many giants in the faith have written amazing books on the topic of the Lord's Prayer, the concept of business and work and thousands of books about man's purpose. This book is not meant to be an exhaustive study on any of these facets of Kingdom life. I am simply inviting you to be a part of one entrepreneur's journey: mine.

Foreword by Pedro Adao

One day, as Jesus was in prayer, one of His disciples came over to Him as He finished and said, "Would you teach us a model prayer that we can pray, just like John did for his disciples?" (The Passion Translation Luke 11:1). In the short time I have to introduce you to this book, the one word I'd like to call your attention to in this verse is, "model." This disciple had the wisdom to ask Jesus to teach them a "model" prayer.

Every successful entrepreneur knows how important and necessary models are. Every successful company must have a sound business model: a process, system or method for how to attract clients and to serve them at a profit. A model provides a framework, a way to organize our thinking and roadmap for directing and aligning our actions. A model helps us stay focused and connected to what is important, what outcomes we want to create more of and what things to reduce or eliminate. In this book, Derek Tye aims to take this model prayer taught by Jesus to His disciples...and illustrate its importance and value to us as Kingdom entrepreneurs.

One of the most well-known challenges faced by entrepreneurs is distraction. Sometimes this lack of focus is referred to as "Shiny-Object Syndrome." It is very common to see entrepreneurs go from thing to thing, going from one opportunity to another or maybe even doing three to four different things all at the same time…hoping that maybe one of these things will be the one thing that they can get to work.

Rarely is this process fruitful. Unfortunately, many people stuck in this pattern confuse business with productivity. Being busy and not seeing abundant fruit is toil, it's a curse, and is not what we are after. As Kingdom entrepreneurs, we should be focused on multiplication and seeing good fruit, positive outcomes in our own lives and in the life of the clients we serve. Therefore, to help us stay focused on the right things…to keep our priorities straight…to keep the main thing the main thing…2,000 years ago, the Lord taught His disciples this model prayer.

As the founder and leader of the 100X Academy, a community for training and equipping Kingdom entrepreneurs, it is of utmost important to stay focused on the right priorities. The Lord has spoken to us on multiple occasions about His priorities for this Kingdom movement He has placed us in charge of:

The priorities of the 100X Kingdom Entrepreneurship Movement:

1. The King

2. The Kingdom
3. The People

Before finalizing any decision both large and small, my team and I run it though this prioritization model. And when we look at this model prayer (the Lord's Prayer), that's the exact same priority we see.

Our Father in heaven, hollowed by Thy name – Priority #1 The King. Your Kingdom come, Your will be done, on earth as it is in heaven – Priority #2 The Kingdom. Give us daily bread, forgives us our debts, and lead us not into temptation – Priority #3 The People

I am so excited for what's possible for you as a result of you investing the time to go deeper into your understanding of The Kingdom of God. I would urge you to not allow the information you are about to learn to remain knowledge. Instead I would implore you to pursue wisdom, which is the rightful application of the revelation knowledge that I believe is available to you in this book. Transformation is a byproduct of application.

I pray that the Lord grants you the grace to understand what, how and when to apply the powerful Kingdom keys available in this book.

—Pedro Adao, Author, Speaker, Founder of Fortress Financial Group and 100X Academy

Introduction

I have always wanted to write a book. When I was about ten years old, I wrote a small book; a one-page guide about how to be a good sales person. My mom was my first and only reader of this book, until we found it years later and had a good laugh. She framed it a few years ago, and today it hangs in my office as a reminder that I am an author. I have a dry sense of humor, so you'd have to read it with a ten-year-old's sense of humor in mind! My mom always told me I would be successful someday, and deep inside I always knew she was right. What I couldn't quite grasp yet, was what my success would look like.

When I was young, I always imagined myself as the CEO of a large company. So when I finished high school, I decided I was going to graduate from college with a bachelor's degree in exactly four years (eight semesters). I did all the math, figuring the most efficient way to graduate with a Bachelor's Degree in Business Management was to maximize my credit hours each semester, taking between 12 to 17 credit hours. Although it's not uncommon for students to complete their degree in four years, I was doing it in addition to working 30 hours a week, getting married and being a homeowner. This time period, between 18 and 22 years old, proved to me that if I put my mind to something, I could make it happen.

As I reflect on that time in my life it seems like a distant memory, but at the same time feels like just yesterday. Although I did not end up becoming the CEO of a large corporation, I did become President of my own company: The Tye Group. I may be President, but God is my CEO! Actually, my wife Jessica and I have started several companies – some are still around and some we had to kill off, but that's for later in the book...

A few years ago, I decided I wanted to write a book. Really, I felt God nudging me to write one. Since then I have been writing notes, doing Facebook live recordings, coaching others and teaching classes in preparation for this project, noticing how God was preparing me for it. During a Kingdom business conference I attended in March of 2019, I met with a publisher one morning and all of the pieces started falling into place. Later that same day, I was at a prayer and prophetic seminar and got a word from the prophet there who I had never met, Matt Gonzales. Matt, not knowing this dream in my heart or that I had met with a publisher that very morning, told me he saw me sitting down, writing a book, with a quill pen, and that it would be a significant work for the next generation. It shocked me to hear this word! Literally it was that *same morning* when I had sat down with a publisher on this three-year journey!

So this was another confirmation from God to *write that book*. Matt's word wasn't the first time someone had told me I'd write a book, but this was the final push I needed. So cheers to this book and the journey it has taken me on to finish it. To me, this effort has been a success **if at least one entrepreneur finds their unique vision and purpose and lives out a new, exciting life and business in partnership with Jesus.**

Success in business can be viewed through many different lenses, and depending on who's looking, it might be either a good or bad thing. To me success has been great (with the counterbalance of my spirit and family life), and I'm really excited to teach other business owners to live by faith and grow in their Kingdom revelation.

It has been said that teaching on a subject is the best way to learn it for yourself, so the message in this book is really also a lesson plan to myself. I'd like to invite you to share the journey along with me. Let's take this journey together, and I hope there is at least one tip I have discovered and share in this book that will help make your life and those around you more successful. This book focuses on The Kingdom of God and how we can take the Bible's principles and apply them to our business lives. In the Bible, it says God is then drawn into the conversation we are having about Him. *God, we invite You into this time together.*

Let's start the conversation with my backstory.

Chapter One

My Story

I grew up on the east side of Cincinnati, Ohio, in a suburb called Glen Este. Our school district consolidated after I graduated, so "Glen Este High School" is no more. If you were to look up that school right now, it doesn't even exist. Oh well. At least we have the memories of school spirit, team colors and hallway shenanigans.

I was born in 1976 to Gene and Jean Tye, and I always tell people I came from good "genes." This is another glimpse into my dry sense of humor. My younger brother rounded out our family of four. We also had two half-sisters and a brother from my Dad's first marriage who occasionally lived with us. From early on, as young as I can remember, my dad worked many different kinds of jobs. Even though he had a successful teaching career in California when he and his first wife divorced, he moved back to Cincinnati where he was raised. It was here where he reconnected with my mom at a 15-year high school class reunion and married soon afterward.

My dad was unable to find a full-time teaching position in Cincinnati, but was able to be a substitute teacher and supplement his income with various sales positions. I even saw him take more humbling positions like driving a limousine for several years to help make ends meet. My dad passed away in 2000, but if there's one thing I remember about him, it was his dedication to generosity. He faithfully tithed to our church on all of our family's income and gave extra to charities he believed in. He would always take food to people who needed it and had a heart for widows, orphans and Native Americans.

My mom was the main breadwinner in our family. She helped shape my thoughts on hard work and discipline (even if she didn't love her 45-minute commute each way to work). She was employed by a big engineering firm and worked with the same group of people for about 40 years. Because of her amazing work ethic and rarely calling in sick, her supervisors took very good care of her. She was well respected. Although she wished she could have been a stay-at-home mom, she made the sacrifice to help the family pay the bills.

Our home was humble by some standards, yet we were happy and I lived there my entire childhood. We had the biggest backyard in the neighborhood, making us the kid-magnet house. All the kids who lived nearby came to play in our yard; the yard with the big trees for climbing and even a dirt volleyball court. I grew up digging holes, building tree houses, playing volleyball, baseball, driving remote control cars around a dirt track we made, and making mud pits. That was a good life for us. My parents decided to sell the house when I was 20. My wife and I got married young, bought the house from my parents and lived there another five years.

From a very young age I remember wanting to be a successful business person. Business and sales was in me. I started by participating in all the 1980's catalog sales opportunities – you know…stuff that you do to raise money for different things in elementary school and mail order catalogs found in the back of magazines. I even did this on my own, going from door-to-door, selling things and keeping track of the money with very detailed records. Charts and tables were my sales tools, even at this early age. Of course now we call those spreadsheets!

I remember going to my neighbors and having some fear that they were not going to want what I had to sell. Fears that they would answer the door and be mad crept up sometimes as I

> *If I believed in what I was selling, I would fill up that order form and get the money I wanted.*

stepped onto their front porches. I also remember the smiles I got and the orders I took from people who were just *happy to help a kid out.* Specifically, I thought if I believed in what I was selling (a discount to a magazine the neighbor was probably already buying at the grocery store for a retail price) and stayed friendly, I would fill up that order form and get the money that I wanted.

Next, I decided to start a business washing hot wheels with the tiny car wash I got for my birthday. I never convinced any other kids to pay me for this, but it was one of my big ideas! I also helped promote neighborhood "events" like a skateboarding exposition that my friends and I starred in with flyers door-to-door and a very low entry fee. Only our biggest fans (our moms) decided to come, and I don't remember if we actually collected any cash.

After my *many* years of experience, at around 12 years old, I wrote a little book about how to be a good sales person. Not the best advice in the world...but it was my start!

Derek's Tips
to a
Successful Business

1. Always keep a smile and act nicely toward your victim.

2. Use manners when speaking to him or her, such as: "Miss," "Sir," "Gentlemen" and "Ladies."

3. Always have a good theme, and not just "I'm selling stuff." Use, "I have a lovely, . . ." "With a coupon for . . .," etc., if necessary.

4. The customer is always right.

5. Have a good cause to tell the customer, such as: "I need to buy my mom a present for her birthday," or "I need to make some money to take me through summer camp."

6. Admit your faults, "I'm new at this," or "I'm sorry for the inconvenience," or "These prices might be a little steep, but, etc. . . ."

7. Business before pleasure.

Derek Tye (age 12)

During high school I decided I didn't want to participate in sports, even though I was generally an athletic kid. Instead, I wanted to be in our school's drama and theatre program. I was the lead in one school play and had minor roles in a couple others. I also extended this fun into my university days by participating in a high-level improv group that toured local high schools with a show.

Because of the plays, I met a lot of fun people, cultivated lasting friendships and made great memories. Theatre also taught me how to memorize a script (which came in handy later for sales positions), how to block (stand in front of an audience when you are speaking), how to think quickly in front of audiences (through the improvisational style of acting). and to project my voice (without a microphone). It also gave me the confidence I needed to say something in front of a large crowd. I have since used these skills to emcee dozens of events ranging from Chamber of Commerce dinners to non-profit fundraisers, one church sermon and many Vacation Bible School kids' events, to Board of Realtors award nights. Thank you to the drama department at Glen Este High School and Northern Kentucky University.

A big part of my story is marrying my high school sweetheart, Jessica, and building an amazing life with her. We started dating when I was a junior in high school, and we were married in 1996, while I was a sophomore at Northern Kentucky University (NKU). Jessica had just graduated from high school, so we were married very young by today's standards. Because of our ages, people told us we might be making a huge mistake, but we just felt that we were destined to be together. Boy, looking back I am so glad we took that chance. We have been happily married since and have five awesome kids and several businesses.

While at Northern Kentucky University I joined a business organization called Phi Beta Lambda and was able to start my first real business networking there. I really enjoyed my business studies and the professors and other motivated aspiring business people and graduated in eight semesters (on the dot) with a Bachelor's Degree in Business Management and Business Administration.

After my graduation from NKU, I did my best to climb the corporate ladder, working for several companies: Hasbro Toys, Cincinnati Bell and US Bank. I realized that as much as I loved being a business person, working for big corporations was not for me. I had all of these crazy ideas to change the products, add new product lines, do radical marketing campaigns and shake up the current business models at these companies.

> *I had crazy ideas to shake up the business models of these big companies.*

While working at the Yellow Pages division of Cincinnati Bell, I remember coming up with an amazing idea. Think back to 2000 when all the companies were racing toward the Internet bubble. I was one of the 20-somethings who thought that this *Internet thing* might actually take off. I proposed a radical idea: since our Yellow Pages company was (finally) rolling out new products to get traditional advertisers to expand their reach to websites and an online search directory, I thought it was only logical they would want to create some radical advertising for the consumers to see the value in using the online search too.

I pitched it to the decision-makers so smoothly... *Imagine a child using a thick Yellow Pages book as a booster seat. They have a laptop computer open, displaying our new "online" version for the next generation, and are showing their mom and dad the new technology.* I thought this was brilliant, and actually I still think this was cutting edge! Unfortunately, the old-school mentality of the day said that the child's *bum* on the sacred yellow pages would be insulting...so they said a big "NO" to my idea.

This kind of thinking and other corporate-minded decision making led to my departure from that company. I also gave the "college try" to the technology and wireless side of the business world...*surely they will be more forward thinking...* but still kept finding the same ideology. In retrospect, I see how the good people I worked with who were in leadership positions were working towards their idea of success, which was most likely pleasing the next level of leadership for raises or promotions. This is where I think I may have been somewhat different than them. This could be one example of the difference between an employee mentality vs. an entrepreneurship mentality.

In my next attempt at climbing a corporate ladder I worked in the banking industry selling products to both consumers and businesses. Sadly, my frustration with corporate

America continued. I remember one day, sitting at the closing table for a commercial purchase deal, seeing the real estate agent receiving a check for around $30k while my bonus for the same efforts was about $350. *Three hundred and fifty dollars? Hmm, I am smarter than this.* Even though I earned a "respectable" salary, about $35K per year at the time, I thought I was better off taking my chances to earn commissions or profits instead.

> *I saw the real estate agent receive a check for $30K, while my bonus was only $350.*

Shortly after, I decided to step out and become a full-time entrepreneur. Since my wife and I had bought and sold a couple of houses early in our marriage (getting married and buying our first house at the same time), I already knew I liked the real estate business. A few years later I also learned how to split/sub-divide land because of the first home we owned and sold. By sub-dividing we made more money selling the vacant lot separately than we would have selling the house with an extra-big yard. I arranged the survey, contacted the bank for a partial lien release, contacted builders in the area to see who may want to buy the lot, and arranged the title work – all of this on my own at about 23 years old. So with a "quick" real estate sales degree added to my resume, I was off to the races as a real estate agent!

I quickly discovered there was plenty of basic training available on how to stay out of legal trouble with your real estate license, but no local real estate sales training matching the business model I was seeking. While at the corporate jobs, I learned a lot about technology, websites, Google and online advertising. I also learned a lot about leverage through people and systems. The majority of real estate agents in 2004 were using very traditional methods to build and maintain real estate sales, including door knocking in neighborhoods, open houses, mailing postcards, hand-written letters, newspaper ads, bench ads, word of mouth, and BNI groups. And, they were all essentially doing this as individual agents, rarely using leverage and systems. Ironically, 15 years later, many of these more traditional paths to real estate sales are still the norm!

When I got started in 2004, I decided to use technology most agents were not, including building a robust website. At the time, this website cost me a small fortune – about $10,000! I had to take out a second mortgage on my house to come up with the money as a newly self-employed person with zero savings. It was a huge risk, but this website became something that set me apart from others in my industry and provided a ton of leads for me to work with. There were so many leads in fact, it allowed me to employ and partner with other agents in my office and sell some of the leads to them. I also discovered that I could keep more traditional office hours if those agents worked with the buyers and I worked with the sellers. More on this later.

This was my first big lesson in leverage! I learned how to win through leverage; leveraging both systems and people. Everybody wins! Partners, clients, my family...

Fast forward 15 years and today we have a robust sales team that has produced, at the time of this writing, over 1,350 sales with over $310 million dollars in sold volume. We have won many prestigious awards over the years. I have been fortunate to serve as the President of the local chamber of commerce and on our local association of REALTORS® board of directors. I am a die-hard entrepreneur and have started more than ten businesses. Some of those ten are actually still businesses!

This may be shocking to some, but over the years I have spent over one million dollars on my businesses. The money went to advertising, websites, promotions, sponsorships, employees, and even on some really dumb ideas that didn't work (some *really* dumb when I look back...). How do I view all seven figures of what I spent? As an excellent education. After all, that is what we really want from money we spend, right? We want to get the best education possible, and in my opinion experience is the best educator.

> *Over the years, I've spent over a million dollars on my businesses.*

Over the last several years, I have been coaching the next generation of entrepreneurs through in-person classes, coaching sessions, podcasts, my Roku network channel, and YouTube videos. This book is another exciting way for me to share with you some insights and learning from those classes.

Beyond my business background, my faith journey is also a significant part of who I am. I grew up in a small, locally run, friendly Baptist church in my hometown where my grandparents and cousins went too. I think my first day in attendance was when I was seven days old. My mom and dad volunteered at the church as ushers and children's church teachers. My brother and I enjoyed going to church as kids, and our family faithfully attended every Sunday (and a lot of Wednesday nights as well). Years later we attended an Assembly of God Church, and then a non-denominational church. Between the three we were exposed to different ways to interpret and read the Bible, various ways to worship and different ways to run a church.

At age five, I asked Jesus to be my Lord, got baptized at 13 and got really serious about my faith when I was about 25. These days I consider "church" to be every day, like when I fire up a faith-based podcast, go to a men's group, attend a marriage small group, have a breakfast meeting (or smoke some meat) with my friend, Angelo, go to church on Sunday, and participate in men's group events.

In real estate, there's plenty of time spent driving around, and I love to listen to audio books and podcasts from ministers in my car. These ministers are from all over the world, and I love the diversity of cultures and points of view. If you are curious about what my favorite books and podcasts are, check out my resources list in the back of the book.

For now, I invite you to come on this journey with me. Let's discover together some insights gained from my interpretation of the Lord's Prayer for us as entrepreneurs. Our Lord, Jesus, has much to teach us. What did Jesus talk the most about? The Kingdom. Why did He talk most about the Kingdom? Because He wanted to align Heaven and Earth now. We are meant to be a part of that.

Key Takeaways:
- Pay attention to what your childhood desires and successes were as a possible clue to your destiny.
- Success can look different to each person.
- We all have different mindsets about work.
- Don't be afraid to try different lines of work or business ventures until you find alignment.
- Know your own story and start paying attention to patterns in your own life and journey so that you can share that with others.

Chapter Two

Why Study the Bible and Involve My Faith in My Business?

Are you aware that many of the Bible's principles seem to be in contradiction to modern business practices? What about the "good life" that many successful business people are striving for and enjoying right now? Do you sometimes wonder if they are doing life the right way, the highest way? I am not here to judge anyone and where they are on their faith journey. Over the years I have been in many places in my own journey...some I am proud of and many I am not. For example, the thousands of wasted hours and at least a good portion of the million dollars in business expenses I wish I could get back.

I also choose to look at those dollars spent as a very valuable education. Thankfully, I have come to know that God redeems our mistakes too. I also like the theme in the New Testament that everything is permissible as a redeemed, saved Christian, but not everything is beneficial to us (or to our business).

As we observe those who appear to be successful business owners, some of them are following Kingdom principles and many are not. Some business experts have coined a phrase for this higher-standard approach to business: "ethical capitalism," where we put others' needs ahead of our own and look to provide massive value to customers.

On the other hand, there are greedy, unethical business people looking to take shortcuts, lie, steal and destroy communities all in the name of profits. These type of business people are the ones making the rest of us look bad. Instead of following biblical principles, they may be following business gurus who are masterful with their sales pitches, leading and manipulating them into shady practices with short term promises of wealth.

This book is an explanation of and an invitation to choose a different way to do business and life; a business and life based on biblical principles using what Jesus talked about the most when He was on this earth: the Kingdom of God.

Jesus was sent to restore what man had lost as a result of the fall in the Garden of Eden. Eden (and Earth as a whole) was created to be a colony of Heaven. This was to be a Kingdom with no sickness, disease, lying, violence, deceit, or lack. This was a Kingdom of abundance. In the Lord's Prayer it talks about God's Kingdom coming here; here on Earth being like it is in Heaven.

Expanding and restoring the Kingdom of God here on Earth takes laborers to make that happen. God has called us to be a part of this restoration process. We are His ambassadors. Do you know what an ambassador is? The ambassador is an embodiment of an entire country. We are called to be representatives of God's country, the Kingdom of Heaven, here on Earth. We need faith to carry out our part of that plan.

> *Vision is a clear mental picture of your purpose*

Part of faith is vision. Do you have a strong vision for your future? Do you have a vision about what your business should look like in five years? Do you know who you are called to serve? Dr. Myles Monroe, the late evangelist, talked a lot about vision in the context of being an entrepreneur. He said that imagination is God's way for us to take a tour of our potential future. He said we all have sight, which is a physical gift from God. But only some have vision, a different and better gift from God. He further defined vision as *a clear mental picture of your purpose*. Stay tuned for more about and from Dr. Myles Monroe later in this book. I believe that you need to come into agreement with this God-given vision for your life and business. I believe God is looking for more of us to come into agreement with Him so we can fulfill His plans here on Earth and expand His Kingdom.

There is a reason you are here. There is something unique that God wanted accomplished through you. No matter what happened with your earthly parents, you are NOT an accident! And if you are alive and reading this, the fullness of that "thing" has not yet been accomplished.

About ten years ago, during my pursuit of success and efficiency in business, I started following Tim Ferris through his podcast and his book *The 4-Hour Workweek*. After reading the book twice, I had a revelation: I needed to work more efficiently. Hiring out for everything I could would allow me to focus on just the top 20% of the daily income-producing activities. I then applied this thought to my personal life, my health and my cooking too. Two of Tim's subsequent books clarified it even more for me, *The 4-Hour Body* and *The 4-Hour Chef*. On his podcasts, I started listening to a bunch of gurus he would interview. Then, I bought their books, their programs, listened to their podcasts and almost joined one of their $25,000 per year mastermind groups. I absolutely geeked out on the idea of efficiency, building a big business, scaling my ideas fast and living life to the fullest in every area!

There was one thing missing though; one *big* thing. My faith journey was simultaneously growing at church and in my quiet study and prayer time. I felt a strong calling and vision to grow a business *and* live by my Christian faith. How did all the guru entrepreneurial advice pair with my deep studies in the Bible? Could faith combine with my crazed entrepreneurial journey? None of the gurus talked about God, or if they did, it was more like how one of my mentors says that some Christian entrepreneurs add "God sprinkles" to their businesses instead of basing the business on Kingdom principles. At the time, I hadn't been exposed to any examples of Christians involved with prophetic ministry who were also simultaneously successful in the business world either. All of my questions led me to more questions, sparking a ten-year quest for answers.

Here are some of things I asked myself. Take a moment to ask yourself these questions and write down the answers:

- Do you know how to build a successful business without feeling like you are selling your soul?

- Do you have a vision?

- Do you know what your purpose on Earth is?

- Do you know how to build a sustainable business that will outlive you?

- Is it okay to be wealthy?

- Is it okay to be successful?

- What is my big *why* and how do I figure that out?

- What is my big *why* in business or for my company/job?

- What is my unique value/gift? What am I good at, and not good at?

- Is it okay for me to work hard?

- What does the "good life" look like?

- Are you ready to trade in the "good life" for the "great life?"

These are some tough questions. I don't have a perfect answer for all of these for myself or for you. Every day I pray for God to reveal answers to me through the Holy Spirit. I am on a journey like you and invite you to take it with me as I grow in revelation and truth.

I am here to give you some good news to help you in the next phase of your journey: the Kingdom is here now! Let's read the scriptures below:

> *"From that time on Jesus began to preach, 'Repent, for the kingdom of heaven has come near.'"* Mathew 4:17 NIV

Repent means to change your way of thinking, to turn and go a different direction. The Kingdom of Heaven is real and it is accessible to you now. Are you willing to change the way you think?

> *"But seek ye first the Kingdom of God and all these things will be added to you."* Matthew 6:33 NIV

That's it! Let's start with the Kingdom. Focusing on God and His righteousness will be my first focus, and all these other things can and will be added to my life (and to those around me). But exactly how do we focus on His Kingdom first when we need to build a business here on this Earth today to pay our bills?

Many business leaders and entrepreneurs wonder how the Bible and their belief in God relates to the business they are also very passionate about. Let me give you the

> *You will not find true fulfillment in life and business without understanding biblical principles.*

honest truth. You will not find true fulfillment in life and business without understanding biblical principles.

To help us get started with the right perspective and thoughts, I am going to share what I have learned from several authors over the years about the Kingdom of God (otherwise known as the Kingdom of Heaven). Both phrases are used interchangeably in the New Testament.

God's Kingdom revelation is a topic I constantly listen to pastors and teachers talk about. My goal is to learn something new every day. I also understand we are each at different places on our faith journey. Some are exploring Christianity, some are new to the faith entirely, some are agnostic, some are atheists, and some of us were in Sunday school from diapers on. To get us all to one common starting place, here are some highlights of the Kingdom of God to help us with the journey. Again, I am not a pastor, priest or Bible expert. This is a simple summary of biblical ideas and concepts about God and Jesus in my own words, in my interpretation and from my personal experiences with the Lord. For us to be on the same page, I want you to know my worldview and beliefs. I encourage you to pray and ask the Lord to give you His truth deep in your soul and get your own unique revelation of who Jesus is from prayer and discernment. In the resources section at the end of this book, I have shared my summary of who God is in an outline. If you want to take a few moments to review that before moving forward, it may be helpful. See page 133.

Now that we have a brief summary of who God is and what His purpose is according to the Bible (in my humble words), let's get started talking about how that applies to our life and our business. Life is really a series of counterbalance moments. For me, I am passionate about many things: my wife, the Kingdom, my kids and business. You probably have a similar list. Have you noticed there are seasons and time periods where one of those passions needs to take priority? This is part of our walk with God too. The Holy Spirit guides and directs us to achieve an optimal counterbalance in our lives.

For example, I wanted to bring the journey and passion I had for business in line with my spiritual and faith journey. I knew there had to be a connection there, so I kept praying, reading, learning and exploring great Christian authors, teachers and business coaches. I was driven to pursue God, and in return He guided me to discover wisdom.

The following scripture is one of my favorites, and I think

it summarizes this concept nicely:

"And we know that in all things God works for the good of those who love him, who have been called according to his purpose." Romans 8:28 NIV

Our personal, spiritual and business lives are more closely connected than we realize. You can't have one without it affecting the other. The good news is that God will use every part of our life to work together for the good of those who love Him. Do you love God? Well, that is a great start. He can redeem our past mistakes, failures and misses. I can personally testify to that. I also love this next scripture:

"Do not conform to the pattern of this world, but be transformed by the renewing of your mind. Then you will be able to test and approve what God's will is — his good, pleasing and perfect will." Romans 12-2 NIV

God's good, pleasing and perfect will is what I want to aim for. If I had to choose, I would choose the *perfect* will, wouldn't you? Why go through life settling for the good or pleasing will? How long would we want good when perfect is available? Well, if we can all agree we want the best, how do we achieve being in God's perfect will?

A life spent getting to know the Creator of Heaven and earth is a terrific start. And, guess what? The very good news is **He wants to do life with you**. A life in line with God's will and purpose for you and your business is sure to be an amazing journey! So rest assured, wherever you are, you are in the right place now.

Here's a handy chart on what seeking God's perfect will looks like, and on the flip side, also what doing life your own way looks like:

Seeking God's Perfect Will Looks Like...	
Life with God leading:	Life with me leading:
True Joy	Temp happiness w/later disappointment
Life	Death
Fulfillment	Emptiness
Sustainability	Short-term success
Abundance	Lack
Life full of quality relationships	Transactional relationships
Peace	Anxiety
Identity in Him	Identity changes as life changes
Acceptance of discipline	Feeling offended
Wealth	Poverty

Do any of these strike you? Which one? What can you do about that?

Have you heard the story of Joseph in the Old Testament? Here is a really quick recap. Joseph is the favorite son of many sons in his family. He tells his brothers about a dream he has in the night; a dream in which his brothers bowed down to him. Did I mention all these brothers were older than Joseph? Yes...and they didn't take kindly to this seemingly arrogant dream. Since his brothers really didn't like Joseph even before this dream, they devise an evil plot and end up selling him into slavery. He is sold to a high official in Egypt, and then a few years later gets falsely accused of a crime. Despite being an innocent man, Joseph goes to jail.

In jail, new friends who Joseph interprets dreams for forget about him when he needs them the most. Miraculously, he is ultimately given a chance to interpret a dream for the Pharaoh of Egypt, which God helps him do accurately. Because of this accurate interpretation, Joseph gets favor beyond his wildest dreams. Pharaoh promotes him to become the second most powerful man in the world. Many years later, his brothers end up coming to Egypt to get food during a severe drought… and there is Joseph…in charge of all the food supply in the region. The brothers end up bowing down to him, literally, not knowing who he was at first.

At one point in the story, God says this about Joseph: "He was a successful man." At what point in Joseph's hero journey did God tell us this? Was it when his brothers were bowing down to him near the end of the story? No! It was just after he was thrown in the pit when he was sold into slavery. That is the moment in scripture where God tells us Joseph was a prosperous, successful man. So my challenge to each of us is this: don't look at external vanity metrics to determine success. From the world's definitions it may not look like you are successful now. However, I believe if we are following God's plan in our lives and are pursuing our relationship with Him, we *are* successful now!

> *If we're following God's plan in our lives and are pursuing our relationship with Him, we are successful now!*

However, I believe if we are following God's plan in our lives and are pursuing our relationship with Him, we are successful now!

This is where identity in God and not circumstances has to be a real, daily goal. What does He think about you right now? I can tell you. You are God's child. He loves you. He wants a relationship with you. He wants you to stop striving for things that He doesn't want for your life. He has a perfect will for your life, no matter what you have done in your past, your present or what stage of business or personal success you are in right now.

I have been gifted with a specific vision of God that has helped me over the last few years. When I used to think about God, I envisioned an old man sitting in a white robe on a cloud controlling the universe. Later in life, I would envision Jesus on a cross, dying for me. Recently someone described Jesus sitting at the last supper with John the disciple curled up in his lap just letting Jesus love on Him, hugging him. Now when I think of God I go to that vision, except it is *me* in Jesus's lap, not John. He was the disciple who Jesus loved, and I know I am too! I know that God loves me and is pleased with me. He knows my heart and that I love Him too.

My dad passed away almost 19 years ago and I miss him a lot. If my dad had the chance to come back to Earth and spend a day with me, I know he would do it. It wouldn't matter if I was having a "good day" or a "bad day." He would come no matter what just to spend time with me in whatever season of life I was in. Our Heavenly Father loves us infinitely more than an earthly father ever could, so I know God wants to spend time with me right now! And with you!

So which stage of life and business are you in? The dream, the pit, slavery, the betrayal, just got your big promotion, or are you standing on a stage receiving applause? Let's take this journey together and see what success looks like at every stage.

> *"You are never too old to set another goal or to dream a new dream."* — *C.S. Lewis.*

The process of bringing a dream into reality is hard…at any age! There are many necessary steps and it can take a while. Remember, however, that purpose needs to precede plans. If you don't have the right purpose, the plans will not be correct. That is one major reason we need to be in consistent fellowship with God. I believe this is done through prayer and listening. So, let's assume for today that you are on your way to discovering your purpose or already have a clear idea of what that is.

Purpose must precede plans

This leads us to planning and goal setting. One of the first big steps is to collect data about our chosen field, get an education and start working in that business area. There are many necessary steps to take over several years. Along the way, helpful and not-so-helpful data enters our brains constantly. If we absorb and retain that data it becomes knowledge, good or bad. If we take it a bit further and really digest and dissect it, the knowledge transforms into understanding. Once we clearly have understanding and take action on it — apply the new data — then it can become wisdom. For myself, I am seeking real wisdom in every area of my life, including building a business and wealth creation.

From this point on we're heading into the meat of the content. Congrats! You have made it this far, so let's keep going. The next chapters explain specific revelations

> *Data becomes knowledge. Knowledge becomes understanding. Understanding becomes wisdom.*

God has given me about building a business using the Lord's Prayer. Why the Lord's Prayer? As I prayed about the book's content, I kept asking God to reveal to me the framework or structure He wanted me to deliver it to you in.

For years I have had journals and notes full of things He has shown me. *Lord, how do I organize all this?* While praying the Lord's Prayer I felt like God showed me that all those notes could be organized into themes found within that prayer. He is brilliant! Those who know me know I carry around a journal almost everywhere I go including conferences, classes and meetings. I am a good student who loves to learn!

Thankfully the disciples of Jesus were the same way. They

followed Jesus around, listened, watched and collected what we now know as the Gospels. At one point they wanted to know how to communicate with Heaven just like Jesus was doing. "Teach us how to pray, Jesus." The disciples asked Jesus how they should pray; how to pray to be the most effective. This is my kind of question! Jesus gives them a short and sweet prayer, yet one full of powerful segments. Most people are familiar with this prayer, even those who don't regularly attend church.

In response to His disciples' question, here was Jesus' answer. Here is the Lord's Prayer spoken by Jesus and recorded by Matthew:

"This, then, is how you should pray: 'Our Father in heaven, hallowed be your name, your kingdom come, your will be done, on earth as it is in heaven. Give us today our daily bread. And forgive us our debts, as we also have forgiven our debtors. And lead us not into temptation, but deliver us from the evil one.'"
Matthew 6:9-13 NIV

Now, starting with the next chapter, I will break down each part of the prayer into segments that we can apply to our businesses. Thank you for going on this journey with me!

Key Takeaways:

- Jesus was sent to restore what man had lost as a result of the fall in the Garden of Eden.
- Data becomes knowledge. Knowledge becomes understanding. Understanding becomes wisdom.
- Vision is a clear mental picture of your purpose.
- There is something unique that God wants to accomplish through you.
- Jesus asks us to repent, to change our way of thinking, to turn and go a different direction.
- The Kingdom is real and accessible to you now.
- Jesus gave us a framework on how to pray: the Lord's Prayer.

Chapter Three

Hallowed be Your Name (Not My Name...)

Why are we trying to become successful? Is it for us or for His Kingdom?

*"This, then, is how you should pray: 'Our Father in heaven, **hallowed be your name,** your kingdom come, your will be done, on earth as it is in heaven. Give us today our daily bread. And forgive us our debts, as we also have forgiven our debtors. And lead us not into temptation, but deliver us from the evil one.'"* Matthew 6:9-13 NIV

What does it mean to hallow God?

Hallowed means respected, honored, holy. We are to give honor to God and respect His name. We are to revere Him. His name is altogether holy. Not only is this a great reminder of how to start praying every day, but also how to start a decision-making process. Googling hallowed's definition brings this statement up first and it seems to do the word justice: "High renown or honor won by notable achievements." Jesus is telling us here to give God the glory.

If you watch the Super Bowl or some big sporting event,

they usually interview the winning quarterback or all-star at the end of the game. Sometimes you hear phrases like this:

"Our team just pulled together."
"Coach really prepared us well."
"I was just on fire today."
"This one is for the fans."
Or my personal favorite...
"All the glory goes to Jesus Christ, my Savior."

I always smile when I hear that last one. Those are all statements of who gets the glory. Some take it all for themselves, some share it and some give it all away. I also wonder about what I'd say if a microphone was pushed in my face in a moment like that. What would I say? I hope I would give God all the glory.

In the business world we usually hear other types of popular accolades, positive and negative, after someone has achieved success.

"He came from money, so no wonder he built that big business."
"He pulled himself up by his bootstraps."
"I am a self-made millionaire."
"She just had a great idea."
"He just out-worked everyone in his field."
"That guy is mega-talented; no wonder he succeeded."
"I started this business with my bare hands."

There are many ways to describe the journey to success. What is yours so far? Jesus asks us to give God the glory, because ultimately God has given us everything we need to be successful. He gave us the opportunities, connections, connections, health, relationships, favor, intelligence, capital, resources, everything! So if it is all His, why wouldn't we also give Him credit for the success?

> *God has given you everything you need to be successful.*

Is it okay to be financially successful?
This is a big issue for a lot of people. This is definitely a hard question, and one that nearly everyone has an opinion about. Here's mine. I believe there are hundreds of scriptures in the Bible supporting the idea that God *does* want us to be successful and prosperous. I believe as we increase in success here on Earth, many other positive things can happen. One obvious area to be successful in is money. You can become wealthy. As God entrusts you with money, you can give to causes, groups and ministries He has put on your heart.

For example, my wife and I have adopted two children. We deeply believe in the cause of the widows and orphans. As we have experienced greater financial success, we have been able to both personally get involved with helping orphans and also help organizations who promote adoption to others. We have helped orphanages and orphans directly and have done service projects and spent our money helping widows. If God wanted us to stay poor, how else could we have donated time and money to these causes? How could we have afforded the adoption costs? Think about this concept in your own life. No money, no way to significantly aid what you (and God) care about.

What cause or issue are you passionate about? The homeless, the poor, the orphans, the widows, single moms, special needs adults, animals, the environment? Who do you think donates money to all of these organizations to fund the work they do? We need money to donate. Maybe you're thinking, "Well, I can donate my time." That does help in small ways, but we cannot even donate our time if we are constantly working just to survive.

Here is another perspective. Ancient Hebrew wisdom promotes the idea that we are to be of service to God's other children. The more we are of good service to His children (customers), they reward that good service with compensation (money). If we are really good at serving, we become really good at making money. Then the next level happens – we start to scale up! Instead of one person serving one person, we learn to serve several people at the same time (more customers). Then we level up again – we learn to have others help us serve even more people (employees). We train some people (managers) to train more people to lead and serve others.

Do you see where this is going? This is a money-making service model (business), and the better the business does to serve others, the more successful that business is going to be. But this isn't all – we get to take that concept to an even higher level. If that company gets people to believe in the mission of serving others and buys into the leadership of that business, then they get to not only be a part of the ownership of that business, but reap in the prosperity of the blessings from the service (investors or stockholders). Then they may also get paid back for their financial investment (dividends, interest or capital gains) from that process.

After that, we get to level up again. What happens to the people (community) around this business? All the other partner business (industries) around that company will also benefit. Real estate development, other service businesses, restaurants, car dealers, landscapers, dentists, and the list goes on and on. This certainly does not sound like the "evil" side of wealth generation to me. As long as the process produces a value for others around the entire transaction, this can be a very good thing for all involved!

So in a short answer, yes, you do need to become wealthy; wealthy not just for yourself as the world would suggest, but

> *"It is selfish to be poor on purpose."*
> *-Jim Baker*

wealthy also for others and your community. Jim Baker, author and pastor, says, "It is selfish to be poor on purpose." I completely agree! When you do donate your time and money, make sure to give God the glory for the ability and privilege to do so.

Is it okay to be influential?

This is a heart issue for sure. I believe as you become successful, people will want to be around you and want to hear more from you. How will you use this influence? Some may use it to sell more stuff. Some may use it to gain power. Some may use it to get the attention of the opposite sex. Some may use it for the glory of God. How do we do that? Well, the more people who are attracted to you, the more influence you have. The more influence you have, the more you can point them in the way of your Savior and God.

You have probably heard the old expression that flies are attracted to honey. People want to be around other more successful people. When this happens, then you have a platform to tell them the good news. Let them know all your success came from God, then you can show them some of the ways you have applied the Bible and your faith to your business.

Sometimes I put so much pressure on myself to succeed that I forget to look around and see I am *already* successful. Saying that may offend you. Sorry if it does. We can all use the term "successful" differently. I feel successful because I have achieved goals in many areas of my life. Am I finished? No! Am I forever satisfied with where I am right now? No! I have set new goals and have a strong vision for my future. Do you know another big benefit of having a strong vision set for your life? It is easier to say "no" to all the good things that come along; seemingly good things that can distract you from the big vision. The stronger the vision, the easier it is to say "no." Vision will help you choose your priorities.

I have had the privilege of teaching lots of classes and emceeing events. After some of those classes and events other professionals in my industry have come up and asked me for advice on how to create better advertising, promotion, make more sales, offer better presentations to clients, etc. As my success in business has grown, it has given me a platform to share not only the tactics and tools for success, but also the big WHY behind what I do. I am not shy about my faith and many people in my business know me for my faith first. Our company abides by the principles of God first, then family, then business. We also live this out in the culture of our business team as much as possible.

How do you know if you are pursuing your own Glory vs. God's?

Finally, it is important to know the difference between pursuing your own goals, dreams and vision and God's plan for your life. I know of only a small handful of successful entrepreneurs who got an exact blueprint downloaded to their spirit on how to build a business. Usually there are a lot of stories of trial and error. For example, I have tried everything from marketing, to sales, to network marketing, car detailing, food service, real estate sales, and software development. Trust me, it would have been way easier if I had discovered at age 18 that I would find the most traction in the real estate business.

Real estate is where I have made the majority of my income and what has led to other successful business ventures, and I certainly could have done without the hassle leading up to it. God did not speak to me with a booming, audible voice from the sky about what career to choose after high school. Either that or I wasn't listening well! Maybe I could have saved years of my life, or maybe real estate at that young age would have been the wrong timing, causing me to quit before I became successful. There is no way of knowing for sure while on this Earth.

What I can say is that over time, I have learned to listen to God's will for my life. As I pursued success and successful living, He has taught me valuable, priceless lessons along the way. The more I focused on my own plans, the money, the influence and my ego, the less I succeeded. The more I focused on Him and His will, the more successful I became. This is the biggest lesson I can share with you.

This comes back to vision. If you get a vision for your life that revolves around obtaining possessions, cars, houses, dream vacations, and status, this is probably not a vision from God. God's visions are for helping those around us and making their lives better. This could be a big business with happy employees, clients, vendors, suppliers, and a thriving community or it could look much smaller. This is your vision! The vision should bring you energy, joy, enthusiasm and passion as you walk it out into your purpose. It should be easy to get out of bed, stay up late and talk about your venture. This should be a big part of your life, but not *be* your life. God still needs to be your focus. At the same time, when you are living your purpose and fulfilling your vision, the worship of God and the business vision you have been given will go hand in hand.

Caution: don't let your business become an idol...

Be careful. Once your business starts taking off and having success, there is a tendency to let that become an idol. There is a natural urge to take pride in the new business and place unequal importance on it. There is definitely a wide spectrum to consider between pride and humility. Although I plan to delve into this topic more in a future book, for now I would say check your heart. Pray and ask God if a certain wish, desire, dream or vision is from Him or from your own ambitions. I would also suggest getting into an accountability relationship with a peer you trust. Have a Bible study or have coffee together every week or two. Check your heart with that person to see if you lean towards the pride side or the humility side. I believe God will reveal that to you if you ask.

Key Takeaways:

- We are to give honor to God and respect His name.
- Jesus asks us to give God the glory, because ultimately God has given us everything we need to be successful.
- God *does* want us to be successful and prosperous.
- God wants us to be in service to our fellow man. The more we can serve others, the more successful we can be.
- Money follows value.
- People want to be around other successful people. When this happens, then you have a platform to tell them (and show them) the good news.
- When you are living your purpose and fulfilling your vision, the worship of God and the business vision you have been given will go hand in hand.

Chapter Four

Seek First His Kingdom (Not My Kingdom)

There is a real Kingdom (government) from Heaven that we need to model here on the Earth; Earth being a colony of Heaven.

> *"This, then, is how you should pray: 'Our Father in heaven, hallowed be your name, **your kingdom come**, your will be done, on earth as it is in heaven. Give us today our daily bread. And forgive us our debts, as we also have forgiven our debtors. And lead us not into temptation, but deliver us from the evil one.'"* Matthew 6:9-13 NIV

What is a Kingdom?

Jesus talks about bringing the Kingdom of Heaven here to Earth. That seems a little strange. First, let's talk about what a kingdom is. There are a few different definitions of "kingdom" in today's dictionaries. I like what Google came up with at the top of my search: "A country, state or territory ruled by a king or queen. Or, the spiritual reign or authority of God." I can't say that any better.

A big part of my understanding about the Kingdom of God came from teachings by Dr. Myles Munroe. Myles Munroe was a well-known preacher who lived in the Bahamas. He had a revelation about the Kingdom of God that had not been talked about much in the world of evangelism. He came out with numerous books and traveled around the world with a very simple message: the Kingdom was here now on earth and we needed to talk about it more!

My wife and I were on a recent trip to the Caribbean and made a stop in the Bahamas to visit Dr. Munroe's church. Tragically, he died a few years ago in a plane crash. I was able to pay homage to this great man of God and met two of his sisters and his nephew. His nephew even prophesied over me and this book while I was still writing it!

Dr. Munroe used to say Jesus had a mission statement. His mission was the arrival of the Kingdom government that was promised by the Old Testament prophets Isaiah and Daniel. Isaiah wrote, "For to us a child is born, to us a son is given, and the government will be on his shoulders. And he will be called Wonderful, Counselor, Mighty God, Everlasting Father, Prince of Peace" (Isaiah 9:6). Daniel says, "The God of Heaven will set up a Kingdom [on earth] that will never be destroyed," (Daniel 2:44). Daniel also prophesied that with Jesus' coming, "He was given authority, glory and sovereign power; all nations and peoples of every language worshipped him. His dominion is an everlasting dominion that will not pass away, and his kingdom is one that will never be destroyed" (Daniel 7:14).

Munroe also wrote that God's original intention on Earth was to establish and extend His heavenly Kingdom, making Earth an extension of Heaven to be ruled first by humans. When Adam sinned, he did not lose a religion, he lost dominion over the Earth. Jesus came thousands of years later as part of God's plan to restore the Kingdom of Heaven on Earth. Jesus' teachings were all about the Kingdom of Heaven, not establishing another religion. Jesus knows there is another invisible government (country) that can come to Earth to solve earthly problems if we invite it. He wants to impart that belief system and wisdom to us. The primary purpose of the Bible is explaining about our spiritual King, His Kingdom and His royal family as mentioned in the points below.

What is living in the Kingdom of Heaven like?

The Kingdom of Heaven is a country with a culture of peace, joy, daily bread for us, forgiveness, love, patience, kindness, goodness, faithfulness, selflessness, respect for all, gentleness, and self-control. These are the concepts Jesus preached about when He referred to the Kingdom. Everyone in this Kingdom should be healed, prosperous and live in abundance.

Who is the ruler of the Kingdom?

In the Kingdom of Heaven God is the ruler. He sets the rules through His laws. He put Jesus in a position of authority over us. Jesus said Himself in John 14:6, "I am the way, the truth and the life. No one comes to the Father except through Me." So as you can see, we have a higher authority to submit to. The closer we align to Him and His way of doing things the more in line with the Kingdom we

| We have a higher authority to submit to: Jesus. |

become. Let's read and align ourselves with some of these key scriptures for Kingdom revelation and breakthrough!

"Do not conform to the pattern of this world, but be transformed by the renewing of your mind. Then you will be able to test and approve what God's will is–his good, pleasing and perfect will." Romans 12:2

"But seek first his Kingdom and his righteousness, and all these things will be given to you as well." Matthew 6:33

"Enlarge the place of your tent, stretch your tent curtains wide, do not hold back; lengthen your cords, strengthen your stakes." Isaiah 54:2

"Now to him who is able to do immeasurably more than all we ask or imagine, according to his power that is at work within us..." Ephesians 3:20

When we align ourselves with Him we are not conforming to the world. By listening to His words and starting to think like He thinks, we will be transformed by the renewing of our minds. I think this is best done in three steps:

1. Pray for revelation from God.
2. Study the Word of God.

3. Get around Kingdom-centered believers to help you walk this out.

What does the Kingdom have in it?
Most people reading this book probably grew up in a democracy with one ultimate authority figure: a president, governor or prime minster who is the top person in charge. They rule for a certain number of years, then pass along that authority to the next elected ruler. This is much different than kingdoms with a king or queen. According to Myles Munroe, a kingdom has many unique characteristics. For a detailed study on this, I would recommend any of Myles Munroe's books on this topic. For today we will just list out each concept for a general understanding as it applies to God's Kingdom:

- Concept of a King: God is the Ultimate Ruler. He is not voted in. He has always been the ruler and always will be.
- Concept of a Lord: Power, authority and influence. The Lord is my Shephard. I shall not want.
- Concept of a Territory: God has a Kingdom in Heaven and wants us to steward that Kingdom here on earth.
- Concept of a Constitution. Fundamental principles to live by and to set up laws according to. It also establishes rights. Ours can be found in the Bible.
- Concept of a Law. We have a set of rules and guidelines to live by found in the Bible.
- Concept of Keys: Jesus reveals to us that there are keys to the Kingdom. When you have a key, you have

authority to unlock information.

- Concept of Citizenship: Having membership and rights to the Kingdom.
- Concept of Culture: The culture of a kingdom is evidenced in how its people behave and serve.
- Concept of Giving to the King: When the King owns everything we are just stewards, so giving is really just handing back over.

Once you grasp the concepts and ideas of a king and a kingdom it will be easier for you to see how it is very different than a religion. Jesus did not come to earth to start a religion; He came to bring the Kingdom of God here to the Earth. He wants His followers to inherit this Kingdom and have dominion over the Earth through colonization of Heaven here. He wants us to be operating on His behalf, to have authority here on Earth. He wants us to use the Kingdom keys to unlock information and wisdom to further His Kingdom. He wants us to be prosperous, as that is one way He gets glory. It's all about establishing His Kingdom.

What is Stewardship?

Once you understand that King Jesus owns everything inside the Kingdom and He allows us to steward His resources, it becomes easier to understand how He owns our ideas, homes, cars, businesses, and relationships. It's all His! He allows us to steward His resources through many different avenues. It is also important to be a *good* steward of these resources. Good stewardship qualifies us for more being entrusted to us. There is a great parable (teaching story) in the Bible that Jesus told about stewardship: the Parable of the Talents.

"For it will be like a man going on a journey, who called his servants and entrusted to them his property. To one he gave five talents, to another two, to another one, to each according to his ability. Then he went away. He who had received the five talents went at once and traded with them, and he made five talents more. So also he who had the two talents made two talents more. But he who had received the one talent went and dug in the ground and hid his master's money. Now after a long time the master of those servants came and settled accounts with them. And he who had received the five talents came forward, bringing five talents more, saying, 'Master, you delivered to me five talents; here, I have made five talents more.' His master said to him, 'Well done, good and faithful servant. You have been faithful over a little; I will set you over much. Enter into the joy of your master.' And he also who had the two talents came forward, saying, 'Master, you delivered to me two talents; here, I have made two talents more.' His master said to him, 'Well done, good and faithful servant. You have been faithful over a little; I will set you over much. Enter into the joy of your master.' He also who had received the one talent came forward, saying, 'Master, I knew you to be a hard man, reaping where you did not sow and gathering where you scattered no seed, so I was afraid, and I went and hid your talent in the ground. Here, you have what is yours.' But his master answered him, 'You wicked and slothful servant! You knew that I reap where I have not sown and gather where I scattered no seed? Then you ought to have invested my money

*with the bankers, and at my coming I should have received what
was my own with interest. So take the talent from him and give
it to him who has the ten talents. For to everyone who has will
more be given, and he will have an abundance. But from the one
who has not, even what he has will be taken away. And cast the
worthless servant into the outer darkness. In that place there
will be weeping and gnashing of teeth.'"*
Matthew 25:14-30 NIV

My interpretation of this parable is simple. God gives us
each abilities, skills, opportunities, resources, relationships, favor, challenges, capacity, intelligence, gifts, and
more. God is referring to these as talents. He gives us these
according to our ability to handle them. Then He tests us
by seeing what we will do with what He has given us. If
we steward them well, we get more and level up in life and
business. If we bury them in a hole, hiding them from the
world, that might be all we ever get. Now, of course, God
is loving, merciful and gracious to us and may grant us
more or a second chance even if we fail. I get that. Yet, I
believe if we want to keep growing in all of these areas and
succeeding at our life mission, we must learn to steward
these resources to the best of our ability. This leads us to
our destiny. TD Jakes says it best.

*"Destiny is not for comfort seekers. Destiny is for the daring
and determined who are willing to endure some discomfort,
delay gratification, and go where Destiny leads."*
—Bishop TD JAKES

How does this work in my business?

So maybe you are reading this and thinking *what gifts do I have to offer?* If so, you may want to take a gifts assessment test to see what strikes you. I would also ask others who know you well what kinds of positive contributions you make in their lives. Take a look at your passions, interests and hobbies and take note of what you learn and do easily. If you have free time at work, what do you gravitate toward doing? When you feel in your best *flow* during your work time, what are you doing? Stewarding your gifts and abilities well in your business is an important key.

One thing I would strongly caution against is pursuing only what you find pleasure in. Most high school commencement speeches talk about following your dreams so you will never "work" a day in your life. Ancient Hebrew wisdom tells us to pursue finding what people need; needs that we can help with. That could still mean you have other passions, interests, hobbies, etc., that you do for fun, but fall in love with helping people and delivering tremendous value, then fall in love with your work. There may be seasons in life where you change your career. You may find more fulfillment with work in new areas of interest, but don't stay in a seeking mode too long. Always find some way to provide value to your fellow man.

> *Pursue finding what people need; needs you can help with.*

For me, I like coaching, leading and teaching the best. For many years I have been doing a million other things as my primary source of income, and I am finally growing into this area for myself. When I teach my energy level naturally goes up (whether I have had coffee or not), and people tend to think I did a good job teaching. When I teach time seems to go by quickly, and I have a hard time staying on the exact topic or with my notes. I love to explain concepts with examples and extra stories.

Despite my love of teaching, it has not been my way of earning a living over the last 15 years. Being a business owner and real estate agent has been my primary income source, with the majority coming from selling real estate. I am very good at it and can really help people in this area to achieve their investment and family goals. Someday though, maybe after writing this book, I can focus more of my vocational time to teaching and speaking.

To me, books with lots of theoretical ideas are really boring and annoying. I like lists, charts and pictures thrown in there, otherwise I have a hard time paying attention. Using lists, pictures, charts and other explanations plays into my love of teaching. Maybe you are a teacher at heart too, and can teach, train or present to others in ways that you enjoy learning.

Here are some practical ways for you to be a good steward with your business skills:

1. Attend mastermind groups with other professionals (maybe even competitors) in your industry.

2. Go to seminars and conferences on topics which you need to grow in and learn more about.
3. Get a business coach to show you where you can grow and to identify your blind spots.
4. Get an accountability partner in your work who you can share your goals with, and have them check in on you to see if you are moving towards these goals.
5. Mentor someone who needs a breakthrough that you have experienced. This can help encourage you too!

Key Takeaways:

- Take time to understand what an earthly kingdom is.
- Take time to understand what God's Kingdom should look like here on Earth.
- We have an ultimate authority to submit to: Jesus.
- Pray for revelation from God.
- Study the Word of God.
- Get around Kingdom-centered believers to help you walk this out.
- King Jesus owns everything inside the Kingdom and He allows us to steward His resources.
- Steward your gifts and abilities well in your business to achieve your destiny.
- Fall in love with helping people and delivering tremendous value, then fall in love with your work.

Chapter Five

Seek His Will (Not My Will)

Let's get the best possible life advice and direction from the source of creation Himself!

> *"This, then, is how you should pray: 'Our Father in heaven, hallowed be your name, your kingdom come, **your will be done**, on earth as it is in heaven. Give us today our daily bread. And forgive us our debts, as we also have forgiven our debtors. And lead us not into temptation, but deliver us from the evil one.'"* Matthew 6:9-13 NIV

Who is the ultimate source of wisdom?
God! This is pretty obvious, but let me prove it. There are 219 references to *wisdom* in the Bible. Many are found in Psalms and Proverbs. The topic is discussed among the prophets and the kings. Here are a few scriptures to set the record straight...and to save some time in looking them all up!

> *"In the beginning God created the Heavens and the Earth."* Genesis 1:1 NIV

> *"God saw all that he had made, and it was very good."* Genesis 1:31 NIV

"In the beginning was the Word, and the Word was with God, and the Word was God. He was with God in the beginning. Through him all things were made; without him nothing was made that has been made. In him was life, and that life was the light of all mankind. The light shines in the darkness, and the darkness has not overcome it."
John 1:1-5 NIV

"If any of you lacks wisdom, you should ask God, who gives generously to all without finding fault, and it will be given to you." James 1:5 NIV

"The Lord gave Solomon wisdom, just as he had promised him." 1 Kings 5:12 NIV

"The whole world sought audience with Solomon to hear the wisdom God had put in his heart." 1 Kings 10:24 NIV

"The fear of the Lord is the beginning of wisdom; all who follow his precepts have good understanding. To him belongs eternal praise." Psalm 111:10 NIV

So to sum up these scriptures, *God created everything.* He made us and He was pleased with the creation. He also wants us to seek Him and His wisdom. Next to Jesus, Solomon was the most famous man in the Bible when it comes to wisdom. How did Solomon get wisdom?

1. He was created by God.
2. He asked God for it.

That's it. How did Jesus get wisdom? Let's check...

"Coming to his hometown, he began teaching the people in their synagogue, and they were amazed. 'Where did this man get this wisdom and these miraculous powers?' they asked." Mathew 13:54

"But they could not stand up against the wisdom the Spirit gave him as he spoke." Acts 6:10 NIV

"So Jesus said, 'When you have lifted up the Son of Man, then you will know that I am he and that I do nothing on my own but speak just what the Father has taught me.'" John 8:28 NIV

"Very truly I tell you, my Father will give you whatever you ask in my name." John 16:23 NIV

So what did Jesus do? He had the Holy Spirit's help whenever He talked. He asked God for wisdom. He let God teach Him wisdom. Pretty simple, right? I think we overcomplicate the whole topic of wisdom.

First, I think many people search for business wisdom in the wrong places. There are a lot of very *successful* business gurus out there who will sell you on a book, a podcast, a coaching program, a seminar series, or a Facebook coaching group. By themselves, there is nothing wrong with learning a trade skill or technique from these gurus. I have learned a lot from secular authors and teachers during my entrepreneurship journey. There is, however, a difference between learning skills and learning wisdom. If you are truly seeking wisdom, it begins with an intimate relationship with the Creator.

How do we communicate with God?

There are tons of great books on this topic. Since we are focusing on business and wisdom here, let's turn our attention to a study on communication with God in relation to our business. One of my best resources for learning about this topic comes from Shae Bynes who hosts the Kingdom Driven Entrepreneur podcast. Over the years I have listened to her bring on countless guests with amazing stories on how they got revelation directly from God on business plans, structure, products, services, business hours, and much more. Last year, Shae wrote a fantastic book called *Grace over Grind*. Her book is a practical workbook on listening to God and working and abiding in His rest instead of constantly striving and grinding out our production.

Some of my best business ideas have come when I was out to dinner with my wife, having a fun discussion with friends or sitting doing nothing on my back porch. Sometimes we feel like we are stuck on a hamster wheel, running as fast as possible to keep up the productive part of our life. God wants us to rest and feel secure in His provision over us.

In order to foster good communication with God, when we pray, we must truly listen too. Listening for His voice is imperative. God can give us an audible voice with knowledge we need, but most times I believe God speaks to us through dreams, visions, daydreams, our

> *Listening for His voice is imperative.*

imagination, our friends, our pastor, or through praise and worship music. Sometimes I get an image, sometimes it is an idea on a business method, other times He will just give me a spiritual "hug" and tell me He loves me.

I want to share with you a prayer I say *out loud* almost every work day before I get started in my office. This prayer reminds me to slow down, cover my family and home in prayer, and then focus on my work life as well. God has been the reason I have been successful in my real estate business.

My personal, work-day prayer:
Our Father, Jesus, Holy Spirit. Thank you!
Praise to You, God. I worship You, I love You.
The universe You created is amazing. I am in awe of Your splendor and majesty.
The earth and everything is Yours! Every relationship I have is Yours!
Let Your Kingdom come and Your will be done on Earth as it is in Heaven.
Give us this day our daily bread. I forgive anyone who has trespassed against me.
Thank you for my measure of Your faith. You are the author and finisher of my faith. Help me increase my measure.

Jesus, thank you for my salvation. Because of You I will live forever.

Holy Spirit, thank you for being my helper, and help me line up Your will with my actions and thoughts.

Create in me a pure heart.

Thank you for my blessed future, favor and promotion!

The 100-fold return is working for me!

Thank you for everything You have given me and my family.

Thank you for my home and country.

Please bless our leaders and give them wisdom in the decisions they need to make today.

Thank you for forgiving my sins. Cover me in the blood of Jesus. Cover my family and homes in the blood of Jesus.

I declare that my friends and their families continue to grow closer to You.

Bless my relationship with Jessica! Keep us young, happy and healthy together!

I declare that Tanner, Max and Parker are great men of God.

I declare that Gabby and Lily are great women of God.

Through You, our real estate business, The Tye Group, is continually blessed.

Please bless our clients and help them achieve their goals.

I declare that Jessica's nutritional business is blessed.

I declare that our 7 Hills business continues to prosper, attract the right people and produce an exponential harvest for us.

I declare that our rental properties will grow in profit and have no drama!

I pray all of our employees and business associates are blessed beyond imagination!

Lord, help me to make wise decisions in my life.

I declare that my mom will stay healthy and happy.

I declare that You will pay off our houses and my family will be completely debt free.

Jesus, I give you all of my problems and concerns.

I declare that I will continue to be healthy, have a flat stomach and a full head of hair.

I believe I receive my healing today!

I declare that we have full protection of our family!

I am your servant leader and continually have a positive impact on Your Kingdom.

Let me see convergence of Your will in my life.

Help me acknowledge Your ways and understand Your truths.

Let me be a light to others, showing Your love.

Give me clarity and clear instructions on what path to take in every area of my life.

Help me make my time, investments and efforts exponentially productive.

Release Your angels to help me accomplish Your goals!

Give me a clear revelation today of what You want me to accomplish.

I declare that I have NO fear!

Let me govern my sphere in Your truth and direction.

Reconcile me with Heaven, reconcile me with You.

Let my children, friends, family and business associates see the truth; see You.

Bless me to bless others.

Help me lead courageously.

Let me to live a great Kingdom-centered life and help shake the nations.

I declare that we will lend and not borrow.

It is by Your power and Your breath that I have success.

Promotion comes from You alone!
Let Your Word be alive in my heart.
Let my plans succeed with Your blessing.
I am the righteousness of God in Christ.
I believe these things are true and will come to pass!
All Your promises are yes and amen.
I dedicate my plans to You, God.
I pray these things in the name of Jesus!
Thank you, Daddy!
Amen

Working 9-5, what a way to make a living!

Early in my real estate sales career I decided to work traditional business hours instead of the typical 9 a.m. to 9 p.m., seven days a week schedule most successful entrepreneurs and real estate agents work. The reason most people work these hours is that making lots of money can be addicting and fun, and most aggressive business owners like to work *a lot*. Maybe you can relate! There is also one other reason. A lot of us have a hard time telling clients "no" and setting boundaries around our personal and family life.

We had to endure a season of sacrificing family time together until our business was more stable. For a couple years I did meet clients whenever and wherever they wanted. I still tried my very best to make all the sporting events and family parties. By God's grace I don't think I had to miss many at all. But I did have to make that time sacrifice for a while until I was able to hire employees and partner with agents to help with the client load.

When you go from a paid salary position with benefits and vacation time to being 100% self-employed with no benefits, vacation or guaranteed income like I did, that was scary! In addition, we didn't have any real money to invest into our new business, so we took out a second mortgage on our home to pay for a website! Remember, this was back in 2004, so free and easy ways to make high-quality, professional websites didn't exist yet.

We really needed God's help on this one. He gave me a cool idea to create a one-stop portal for all the listings in my hometown of Cincinnati, Ohio...all 15,000 of them. He showed me through ideas how to connect a public site to my personal one, and I got some coding help to make all of this happen. What was the result? We had scores of real estate buyers contacting us through our website; buyers we had never met who wanted information on homes we were not the listing agents for. This is pretty much how Zillow started their business several years later.

These "leads" needed people to show them homes in the evening after work and on the weekends. My commitment to my family was to work as much from 9-5 as possible so I could be home to have dinner each night and be there for sports practices and games. Because of our large number of leads, I was able to ask other agents in my office if they wanted to run buyers around for showings and split the commission, enabling me to be home during those hours.

It was perfect!

The indirect result was a sales "team" that I still run 15 years later! The abundance of leads led to people who I could partner with. The income from those sales allowed me to hire an assistant to do all the paperwork, creating more leverage. I was able to

> *Partnering with others has allowed me to serve a lot more clients than I could have alone.*

work more with sellers, on the listing side of the business, which makes it easier to control my time. Buyers' agents showed the properties and I was able to be home for dinner most evenings by 6:00. Rarely have I missed a game or practice all these years. Additionally, partnering with others has allowed me to serve a lot more real estate clients than I could have alone, and our team has now sold over 1,300 homes. Glory to God!

Saying "NO!"
Over the last 15 years of being a full-time entrepreneur, I have been invited to do volunteer work with various organizations. Serving alongside some amazing people during that time has been a wonderful experience. For my local board of REALTORS®, I went from committee member to chair to Vice President to President and on the board of directors. Simultaneously, I went from Director to Vice President to President of our city's chamber of commerce. At the same time, I was also on the leadership team for our men's ministry at our church. Did I mention we were also hosting a small group at our house during the

same timeframe? Of course this is in addition to all the activities my wife was involved with. Having five kids, a loving wife, a business, close friends, sports activities, church activities, plus volunteering, has made our life very busy.

About a year ago, I was meeting regularly with my business coach Steve Eklund, an amazing Spirit-filled, Kingdom-centered business coach. He was encouraging me to take an inventory of all the various activities I was involved with. The list was long. They were all "good" causes of course, and it was hard to think about what was best for me in my personal mission. After much prayer and discussion with Steve, I decided there was a book I really wanted to write and a coaching program I wanted to start, but they were never going to happen with all these other activities consuming my time. Because of these goals I started strategically exiting out of some of those responsibilities. With God's help the transitions have all gone smoother than I thought, and people were not disappointed in me like I thought they would be. Because of making this shift, I have been able to really focus on this next chapter of my life including writing this book you are reading now!

Where do we get wise, earthly counsel?
I believe we should get wise, earthly counsel from several sources. First, you can seek many wise counselors who have your best interests in mind and have a Kingdom revelation. The Bible tells us in Proverbs to seek wise

counsel, and how there is safety in a multitude of wise advice.

Years ago, one of the hardest decisions I had to make was whether or not to sell and downsize from a dream home my wife and I had built and go rent a home for a while until our finances improved. We thought this house was our forever home. It was fantastic…we built it on some land, added a nice barn, put nice appliances in it, finished the basement, and even dug out a fishing pond. Not all of these are typical projects a person would do to try and sell a home to make money, but we didn't think we would ever sell that house! Although those things were expensive, they didn't necessarily add a ton of value to the property.

As the real estate market (and economy in general) went through a slowdown, a downturn, and then big recession, our income fell for three consecutive years. The value of the home also dropped and the mortgage payment got harder and harder to make, until finally we were left with a very difficult decision: to sell.

So this is where having good counsel came in! My personal instinct was to wait out the market, make a recovery and try and make it all work. Deep inside I think I just didn't want to give up on this dream I thought I wanted. We consulted our pastor, a good friend, my mom, our banker, and an attorney. They all confirmed the same message, and so we sold our home. It was a sad day, that day we all moved out, and our family was upset. Surprisingly there was also a big sense of relief when it was all over. We then rented a home a third of the size in a nearby town.

Looking back at it, I am very grateful we took the advice of the wise counsel and God has been so good to us since. Even though at the time there was a lot of discomfort, we have realized that it was not really our dream after all. We have since bought and sold a few homes and are back on our way to owning and developing a "dream" property again for our family in an even better location.

The first wise counsel I would recommend getting for business and life is your spouse (if you have one). They should know you better than anyone. They will also know how a decision you are about to make is going to not only effect you personally, but also your marriage, family and finances. You can pray together and will have to live with the decision you both jointly make. I also feel like my wife, Jessica, has great intuition and discernment when it comes to people. She can usually pick up on someone's true motives and character better than I can. She may say something like, "I am getting an uneasy feeling about that person, so just take it slow in that business relationship." By the way, she has never been wrong on that! I highly recommend having a spouse to support you like Jessica does for me!

The second counsel I would seek is a trusted friend. Please start investing in great Christ-centered friendships *now* long before you need the critical advice they will provide.

Start building into their life and they will build into yours. As little or big decisions come up, bounce them off that friend and get some good, honest feedback. I have had friends tell me to back off some of my big business decisions and not to step in that direction. The advice ended up being very timely and accurate. I had another friend tell me to focus on my real estate business when what I really wanted to do was just write my book. That was good advice too. So it just took me a while longer to write this.

> *Invest in Christ-centered friendships now.*

I also like to help my friends when they ask me for advice. Angelo is a friend like that. He has given me wisdom, encouragement, direction and tough love, and I have given it right back. He also can smoke some serious pork butt, so I have really learned a lot from him on decision making, spiritual discernment, perspective and cooking. I highly recommend having an Angelo in your life!

Third on the wise counsel must-have list, is a business coach or mentor. These are people you really look up to and who probably have more experience than you at whatever the topic is. These people have achieved victories in areas that you aspire to. Has this person climbed a mountain, build a successful business, written a book, won a fishing tournament? Whatever you are trying to achieve there is probably someone at your church who has already done that. I remember meeting with a mentor once who I highly respected. He had achieved a high level of both personal and business success and had a great reputation in town. We met once for lunch and he asked me a profound question: "When was the last time you got down on your knees before God and really prayed?" Admitting it had been awhile, I got a little more clarity on the importance of doing that more often in the future. I appreciated the advice.

I have had business coaches for the last several years. Each time we connect I learn more about myself and have someone to point out my blind spots. Specifically, a good coach does all of these things and more:

1. Helps you discover what you really want.
2. Helps you get clarity on how to quantify that goal.
3. Helps you get clarity on how to achieve that goal.
4. Gets you encouraged to do the work.
5. Holds you accountable.
6. Repeats the process over and over!

Steve, who I've already mentioned, has been a business coach for me in the past and did a great job helping me build my life to where it is today. I highly recommend also having a Steve in your life!

Last but not least, we have pastors and ministers. A lot of people in church don't feel comfortable calling the pastor or one of their assistants and asking for help. Sometimes you should though. Maybe meet them for coffee or lunch, or just meet at the church office. This is a great way for you to have another person feeding into your life, showing you what God has in store for you. You can also ask them to pray for you; prayer support for clarity and courage, which are my two favorite prayer requests.

Pastors have not only prayed for me for these things, but they have also helped me walk out some life transitions in my business and calling. I'm thankful when my pastor can take my call in the case of a family emergency or meet me for lunch just to check in on all my crazy business ventures! I highly recommend having a pastor like this in your life.

Do you have examples of following God's will versus your own?
God's will might look like a lot of different things at different times. I think most people think you have to give all you have to the poor, living poor yourself in order to see the Kingdom of God. I *highly* disagree. God has given us all unique gifts and favor in different business and ministry opportunities. He has also given us a heart to serve people in unique ways. God's will for you may be making a ton of money selling chicken nuggets and supporting a homeless ministry with the profits. He may have you selling shoes to people in the United States and sending free shoes to people in Africa. He may have you selling homes in Ohio and supporting the cause of orphans in China. Who knows? Someone needs to make some big money to support big Kingdom work. Why not you?

This is our God. We all will have something unique to offer

Him and the world around us with our lives. This is called a *living sacrifice*. I believe that when you discover your unique calling it won't even feel like work. And, the money won't matter so much anymore either. My wife and I really don't care about how much money is in our bank account. Yes, I like to have enough in there to pay the bills and have some savings. However, the number of extra zeros in the balance does not really excite us. Doing something significant and what the future holds is more exciting than money. When we are living our Kingdom purpose here on earth, we know there are some really cool things we are going to get to do!

Have you ever heard teaching that talks about our society having seven main spheres of influence? For the past decade I have been reading and listening to information on this concept. It fascinated me. It made me realize each of us has a segment of society that we are meant to have a career in, influence and serve.

There are seven major sectors — spheres of influence — in the world today. Most Christians think there is only one truly important mountain: the Church. They think they need to become a pastor, a deacon or head up a church committee to be valuable to God. That is not accurate. The truth is that the other six mountains (or spheres of influence) are also where God wants His sons and daughters to operate in authority. He needs His people everywhere.

The other six spheres (other than Church) are Family, Government, Education, Media and Entertainment, Arts, and my favorite, Business and Economy. God wants us to not just run the Church sphere, but to go out into all the world and make disciples in our given field (or sphere) of favor. More teaching on your field of favor to follow!

So in summary, follow God's will for your life. Follow wise counsel and surround yourself with Kingdom-centered people. Then eagerly anticipate what God is going to do next!

Key Takeaways:
- Seek His will (not our own will) by asking for and seeking wisdom from God.
- Jesus had the Holy Spirit's help whenever He talked. We need it too!
- Start with an intimate relationship with God.
- Be willing to say "no" to good things while in pursuit of great things. Ask for God's direction on this.
- Surround yourself with wise counsel to help you with decision making. Start with a spouse, friend, coach and pastor.

Chapter Six

Give Us This Day Our Daily Bread (Not Tomorrow's)

Have an abundance mindset, not a scarcity mindset.

*"This, then, is how you should pray: 'Our Father in heaven, hallowed be your name, your kingdom come, your will be done, on earth as it is in heaven. **Give us today our daily bread.** And forgive us our debts, as we also have forgiven our debtors. And lead us not into temptation, but deliver us from the evil one.'"* Matthew 6:9-13 NIV

What did Jesus mean by *daily bread*?

In the Old Testament of the Bible, God provided for the people in the wilderness by providing manna. The Israelites were in the dessert for 40 years and they had a meal every day. Manna was a wafer-like food that appeared on the ground each morning, except on the Sabbath day (their commanded day of rest). If they collected more than one day's worth of provision it would rot by the next day. Those who collected more, saving it for tomorrow, were subconsciously saying, *I don't trust You enough to feed me tomorrow, God, so I'll make it happen myself.* The only exception was on the Sabbath, when the food from the day before would not rot out. They were directed to collect a double portion the day before the Sabbath.

God sustained the Israelites, literally, with daily bread. What is sometimes lost in this part of history was this shocking thought: the clothes and shoes of all these millions of people never wore out. There were no malls in the dessert! Not only did God provide them with meals every day, he sustained the clothes and shoes for 40 years too. This is miraculous. My kids wear out shoes in four months!

We also see this daily bread concept echoed in Jesus' direct teaching. This is one of my absolute favorite teachings found in Matthew chapter six, so please read and think about what Jesus is saying to you and me here.

"Therefore I tell you, do not worry about your life, what you will eat or drink; or about your body, what you will wear. Is not life more than food, and the body more than clothes? Look at the birds of the air; they do not sow or reap or store away in barns, and yet your heavenly Father feeds them. Are you not much more valuable than they? Can any one of you by worrying add a single hour to your life? And why do you worry about clothes? See how the flowers of the field grow. They do not labor or spin. Yet I tell you that not even Solomon in all his splendor was dressed like one of these. If that is how God clothes the grass of the field, which is here today and tomorrow is thrown into the fire, will he not much more clothe you — you of little faith? So do not worry, saying, 'What shall we eat?' or 'What shall we drink?' or 'What shall we wear?' For the pagans run after all these things, and your heavenly Father knows that

you need them. But seek first his kingdom and his righteousness, and all these things will be given to you as well. Therefore do not worry about tomorrow, for tomorrow will worry about itself. Each day has enough trouble of its own."

I can't emphasis strongly enough how important this passage is. Many of us have grown up with some form of poverty or lack in our family. Maybe we didn't get the toys for Christmas we really wanted as a child. Maybe you have a memory of going hungry a couple of meals. Maybe your family didn't have the funds to buy you new clothes, so you always wore hand-me-downs. My mom and dad didn't make a ton of money, but thankfully always provided for us. They were masters of frugality and we definitely had hand-me-down clothes from older cousins.

> *Many of us have grown up with some form of poverty or lack.*

I even remember wearing some "tighty whitey" undies as a kid with a cousin's name written on the waist band. The funny part of the story is that it was a second cousin who I had never met. The name was written in black magic marker, and I kind of thought it was cool, like wearing ones that said "Calvin Klein." Years later when I was an older teen at a family reunion, I was introduced to this Calvin Klein undies guy (my second cousin, his name will be withheld to protect the innocent...). My mom poked me with her elbow in my side and said, "That is _____ right there. You used to wear his underwear!" We all had a good

85

laugh, and it made me appreciate what we have and how my mom and dad always provided for me.

Jesus promises us in this passage that we do *not* need to worry. Start singing it right now, "Don't worry, be happy!" Good luck getting that song out of your head now. You're welcome!

God clearly tells us that our Heavenly Father knows exactly what we need. Have you ever seen a bird worry? I can't remember seeing that. You know you are more valuable to God than a bird, right? You are. Trust me! We also see here that worry will not add one hour to your life. My wife is a leading nutritionist in her industry, and she will tell you that worry actually cuts your life short, making you sick while you are alive. So the key is to not worry and know God has your back. He is looking out for you. He loves you.

> *Worry cuts your life short, making you sick while you are alive. Don't worry, God knows what you need!*

If God knows what you need and He says not to worry about our needs, then why do we spend so much time in a worry-riddled mindset? I think we are actually *not* worried about what we will eat or drink or wear today. I think the majority of people's worries are spent worrying about *tomorrow*! And the next day, and the next. In my opinion that is where worry really gets us: fear about the future.

Re-read Jesus' last point of the Matthew six verse I included. If we can spend time trusting God today, letting Him "worry" about tomorrow, we will be much happier today and will live longer, healthier lives! Let's live in faith (in God's ample provision) and not in fear (worry about tomorrow), okay?

How do you know if you are operating in faith or fear, scarcity or abundance?
This brings up a great question. Are you aware of how you are feeling? Here are some things that have helped me become aware of my mindset, beliefs and thought patterns, and maybe these will help you to become aware of fear, worry and scarcity too. Take an honest inventory and see if you resonate with these things.

1. Not tithing or donating money to charity because you feel like you will never have enough
2. Saying things like, "You never know when you are going to need it," referring to how big your savings account is (but it's never big enough).
3. Thoughts like *if I could only have $x in my 401k, then I would feel secure...*
4. Thinking or saying, "If I could just earn $x more per year, then we would be good."
5. Living paycheck to paycheck for longer than a transitional season in your life.
6. If you are obsessed with frugality to the point that you make everyone around you miserable (sorry to offend some of you).

7. If you tend to hoard and have your basement, garage or extra storage places filled to the brim with things you don't need.

8. If you won't lend out your tools, equipment, money, stuff, etc., because you think you may never see it again.

9. Not sleeping at night because you are worried about the next day not having enough, doing enough or about some other repetitive fear.

10. You won't share your business ideas with others because you are afraid they will steal them.

What are types of daily bread that we can see in our everyday lives?

I believe God provides us with everything we need. Most of us focus on the easy needs that have been mentioned above, including money, clothing and shelter. But what about the plethora of other areas God provides for us in? Here are just a few examples:

- New clients for your business.
- Finding key employees who want to work for you.
- Provision for safety/protection in your business.
- Safety and protection for your family.
- Key relationships to help you grow in your business and personal life.
- Grace with mistakes you have made in your business.
- Favor with key clients and vendors.
- Time savings and efficiency.
- Finding wise counsel.

My point is to look around every day and take inventory of the many blessings you already have (even what tragedy you avoided). This is why having a gratitude journal is important. My goal every morning is to give gratitude and thanks before I start my work day. I write all of the gratitude entries into one place and sometimes go back and look at past victories and gratitude when I am having a "bad" day. This has been really helpful for me. I look back and see the victories won in a lot of the areas I am stressing about. It reminds me that God is faithful and He cares about even my smallest needs.

What can we do in our business to serve others without asking for money immediately?
In business we have been taught to make the most money possible. Maximize profit. Take every client. Win every sale. Increase margins and charge more for our service. Get repeat sales. Get referrals. These are all good things, yes. According to Wikipedia, "Capitalism is an economic system. In it the government plays a secondary role. People and companies make most of the decisions and own most of the property... The means of production are largely or entirely privately owned (by individuals or companies) and operated for profit."

What we are learning here is a different government system called a kingdom. In the Kingdom of God we operate under a different set of rules. Instead of money, we prioritize the love of people. People are more valuable than money. As we often discuss in one of my business mentoring groups, "Money follows value."

> *Money follows value.*

What does this *money follows value* phrase really mean in business? If you provide value to people and love them unconditionally first, then you are more likely to later serve them with a monetary reward. Here is an example. In my real estate business, I have received calls from people who want to sell their home. They tell me they want someone to come out and take a look at their house and give them advice on what improvements to make to get the home ready for market. "Sure," I say, always asking them how soon they want to list the home. Sometimes it may be a year or two away. If I was a pure capitalist I would either refuse the request, thinking that the potential payoff is too far in the future, or ask the homeowner for a fee to do this service.

There is nothing inherently wrong with either strategy. What I am proposing is that we "repent" and think differently. Instead, I will go out and give them 100% of my attention. I evaluate the property and give them a list of repairs to make, along with my estimate of market value should they make these improvements. The total investment of time is about three hours. What do I get paid? Nothing, at least for now.

I will then follow up with that potential seller every three months forever to see if they are ready to sell. Sometimes the seller sells three months later. Sometimes it takes three years. At times I have also been disappointed to hear that the seller has decided to take my advice on staging and pricing, but then sells it "For Sale By Owner." And yes, that hurts! No one likes doing something for nothing, especially in a business context. Sometimes I am rewarded with revenue, sometimes I am rewarded with life experience, either way I win. That is part of my mindset. I have to be willing to see no monetary reward for the opportunity to do business with a new client and simply build a new relationship.

I have also taught classes to other agents in my industry to help them build up their businesses. This may seem crazy to some that I am teaching my competition to do a better job at competing against me. If you view this only through the eyes of a pure capitalist, yes, this would make no sense. Instead, in the Kingdom of God we find ways to serve God's children. It's true, some of those children may actually be your competitors today.

There has been fruit from this teaching, such as good relationships with other agents resulting in smoother transactions for my buyers or sellers because of the favor from the other agent who I once had in a class. I have also had agents want to join my real estate company or team after attending my classes. These are nice benefits, but not the main reason why I teach others.

What are other ways you can serve others in your business without making money immediately?

1. You can teach a class to potential clients or other professionals in your industry.
2. Try joining a trade association and volunteering amongst your peers on a board or committee.
3. Run a mastermind group in your industry.
4. Offer free consultations before someone starts paying.
5. Have "taste and see" offers.
6. Offer a 100% money back guarantee.

Of course, all of these come with pros and cons and each one could spark a chapter for a future book!

How do we change our mindset about provision?

Okay, so now you are (hopefully) convinced that we need to lead with love in our businesses. We should also stay committed to producing a high-quality product or service to strive for excellence in building our brand, products and team. But how do we keep the mindset that says *there will always be enough*? Well, I believe this starts with renewing our minds daily. We do this with prayer, meditation, reading our Bibles and sticking with Kingdom-driven friends and mentors. We will also need to operate with a healed heart, and that is what we are diving into next.

Key Takeaways:

- Have an abundance mindset, not a scarcity mindset.
- God will provide you with what you need for today.
- Don't worry about tomorrow.
- Worry actually cuts your life short, making you sick while you are alive.
- In the Kingdom of God, we operate under a different set of rules. Instead of money, we prioritize the love of people.
- Sometimes I am rewarded with revenue, sometimes I am rewarded with life experience. Either way I win.
- Find ways to serve others in your business without making money immediately.

Chapter Seven

Forgive Us Our Trespasses and Forgive Those Who Have Trespassed Against Us (Both, Not One or the Other)

Operate from a healed heart, not scarred or broken.

> *"This, then, is how you should pray: 'Our Father in heaven, hallowed be your name, your kingdom come, your will be done, on earth as it is in heaven. Give us today our daily bread. **And forgive us our debts, as we also have forgiven our debtors.** And lead us not into temptation, but deliver us from the evil one.'"* Matthew 6:9-13 NIV

How does unforgiveness show up in business life?

Maybe you had a rough childhood and blame your parents for that tough start. Maybe a friend hurt and betrayed you. Maybe a business partner stole money from you. Maybe a church representative abused you. Maybe a spouse left you. Maybe your child disappointed you. These debts or "trespasses" against us can leave us with scarred hearts.

We all have tragedy, disappointments and trials that others

may never understand. We all carry hurt and despair. We all have the tendency to struggle with forgiveness and forgetting what has happened in our past. This is something Jesus warns us about in this key prayer. *Forgive us our trespasses* refers to us first asking God to forgive us for our sins. This is huge. Secondly, He wants us to forgive others for the hurt they have caused us. If we carry hurt around into our personal life, it will definitely show up at work too.

People think they can leave all the personal drama at home, keeping their mental and emotional "business box" separate from everything

> *Unforgiveness is like drinking poison and waiting for the other person to die.*

else, but that is nearly impossible. Everywhere we go, there we are, hurts and all. We are not robots, but people with emotions and feelings. I am generally someone who gets over hurt pretty quickly, although I also understand it may take others longer. I have heard that holding on to unforgiveness is like drinking poison and waiting for the other person to die. With unforgiveness we kill ourselves inside.

What is a healed heart?
A healed heart is one that has been hurt then healed. This is Jesus' goal for us, knowing, "It is impossible that no offenses should come," as He says in Luke 17. Life comes with offenses and trespasses. We are healed when have asked God to forgive us for our sins and have forgiven

others for those wrongs committed against us. We are no longer fostering or producing bitterness, negativity, scarcity, anger, jealousy, resentment, or worry. We can then show up with the fruits of the Holy Spirit instead – good, healthy fruit!

What fruits are produced by a healed heart?

I would make the argument that a healed heart produces fruit of some kind, as in the fruit of the Spirit. This list is found in the New Testament:

> *"But the fruit of the Spirit is love, joy, peace, forbearance, kindness, goodness, faithfulness, gentleness and self-control."* Galatians 5:22 NIV

If you can bring all of this kind of fruit into your business life, what would that do for you? How would you treat your employees? How would you handle a key vendor when they need extra attention? How would you attract new clients and retain current clients? How would this affect your marketing efforts? How would this affect your planning and forecasting? Let's look at a few examples.

How can some of these fruits show up in business?

How would love show up in your business? Maybe a local charity you love to support becomes a focus in your meetings. Our company has served as volunteers and donated money to two different charities in Cincinnati. For both organizations, our team has taken time out of our daily work and spent time volunteering. Some of us have also donated money to those charities. This has been a great bonding experience inside our company, and team members talk about these times fondly. It reminds us that our efforts at work are not done in a silo. They affect not only those around us at work, but our communities and families as well. We all need this reminder regularly as we tend to set up selfish existences when left to our own desires.

Also, it is important to fall in love with your clients and employees. If you can't love them you should find another business. I am *not* talking about romantic love of course, but loving someone as a person, knowing they are a child of God. Recently I had a really challenging buyer. Every day when he called my skin crawled and I got a little frustrated. I kept praying about it and God told me very clearly in my spirit that this guy, let's call him Doug, was His child and He loved him. That changed my perspective. So here is what I did to cement in that new thought. In my iPhone I changed the buyer's name to "Doug, The Child God Loves." Then whenever he would call, I would remind myself of that before I answered the call.

How would joy show up in your business? How about making it a marketing tagline that turns into a declaration? My real estate team has a promise to our clients: "More Joy, Less Drama." We say this and mean it. The last thing I want in my real estate deals is drama, but inevitably there is always some speed bump (or six) in there. Each transaction is very unique – some deals have a crazy amount of drama and some have almost none. Either way we do our best as a sales and administrative team to shield our clients from the drama as much as possible. That means doing our best to solve problems as they arise first, without involving the clients until we have at least a proposed solution. Sometimes we just get it done and let them know later to keep the stress out of their world as much as possible.

On the joy side, we always try to do something a little extra special in the transaction to help the buyer or seller feel some joy. Buying and selling a home (and moving) is usually one of people's most stressful events in life. Moving usually accompanies some other stressful event that has spurred the move, like a job change, birth, death, divorce, marriage, parents coming to move in, or kids leaving the nest. All these are potentially crazy times in people's lives. Maybe we give a gift or help out in an unexpected way. Maybe it is an introduction to a new friend or neighbor. Maybe it is a recommendation to a new favorite restaurant! So let's have more joy with our work and business, as much as possible, which helps our clients have more joy too.

What about peace - how would peace show up at your business? Do you have deadlines? Do you like to cram as many activities into your workday as humanly possible? Do you like to make promises to as many clients as you can so you can keep building your

You earn respect when you can stay calm and keep things moving forward.

business bigger and better? Most entrepreneurs do. Problems and drama arise all the time in most businesses, no matter what you do. If it wasn't hard, everyone would be doing your business, right? At least that is what my mom told me. So this is where peace comes in. If you can keep calm and not get rattled every time a problem pops up, people start looking at you differently. You earn respect when you can stay calm and help keep things moving forward. This is something I really like to think I am good at. This comes from the peace of God. He has gotten me through and has helped me solve so many problems.

I have had urgent calls come in from an agent who is representing the other side of a real estate transaction who is yelling about some new emergency issue that has to be solved *right now*. I have listened, told the other agent I would work on it, hung up the phone, stayed in peace and prayed about it. Maybe it required asking another agent or my broker in the office how we can solve it. After brainstorming some ideas, sometimes the issue gets resolved before I have to call my client to explain. Those are the most fun scenarios. That peace that passes all understanding is so cool. I just have to stay cool too.

We also have to be at peace with and have some contentment in the number of clients we are serving. More is not always better and sometimes we need to experience peace in the amount of business we have, especially if serving more clients is going to continue a trend of time spent away from family or friends. Sometimes it is okay to squeeze additional clients in the workload, and sometimes you are already hitting goals but have a hard time saying no to one more deal.

I also know that there are seasons for harvesting business in different industries. In our real estate industry, spring and summer time are the busiest, as people want to move when kids are out of school. This also means we may have to take on a larger workload and meet people earlier or later than our normal schedule would tell us to operate. We then have to counter balance those times when things are slower, like around Thanksgiving, Christmas and New Year, when the calls from clients to list their homes slows down. Sometimes I need to remember to take a little time for myself and my family to compensate for those late nights at the office in the summer time and not stress out that I don't have a lot of clients at that time.

Now it is your turn. How would the other fruits show up in your business? Write a few ideas down.

How would forbearance (patience) show up in your business? This is probably my biggest challenge!

How would kindness show up in your business?

How would goodness show up at your office?

How would faithfulness show up in your business?

How would gentleness show up in your work?

How would self-control show up in your business?

How can I work on making these fruits part of my daily business and personal life?

Well, this is my favorite answer: God and Holy Spirit will help you bear and produce these fruits. You *cannot* produce these fruits sustainably or authentically over time without God's help. That would be impossible. He is here for us. He is here to give us direction every day, every moment. He helps us produce good fruit. He is the source of good fruit. Can we find a scripture to support this? Of course!

"I am the vine; you are the branches. If you remain in me and I in you, you will bear much fruit; apart from me you can do nothing. If you do not remain in me, you are like a branch that is thrown away and withers; such branches are picked up, thrown into the fire and burned." John 15:5-6

I love this scripture! Apart from Jesus we can do nothing! We can try our very best to be a *good person*, and despite our best efforts always come up short. We can try to be the best business person who ever walked the earth and try to keep all the commandments in the Old Testament. We can attempt to love everyone (in our own love strength) and always be perfect. Yeah, right. Just think of that last frustrating traffic jam you were in. That is not going to happen! That is why it is important for us to "remain in Him."

You may be wondering, "How can I remain in Him?" Let's go to another one of my favorite scriptures for that answer.

"If you remain in me and my words remain in you, ask whatever you wish, and it will be done for you."
John 15:7 NIV

This verse is both instructions and a promise. My interpretation of this is that we need to pray and ask Jesus to forgive us of our sins. We need to ask for His instructions in our life, for His way of doing things. We need to read His words and be obedient to what they say. If we do this, He offers us a promise that we can ask in His name and whatever we wish will be done for us. This is where a bunch of really religious people are going to get hostile. I know, I have seen the comments on Facebook pages and in forums. They say you *can't* ask for whatever you want. However, I believe you *can* ask for whatever you want.

Here's some clarification: your request will not come to pass unless the thing you are asking for is what you have faith to believe and you are fully aligned with God in what you want. So there are two parts: knowing the *right things* to ask and *having the faith* to really believe they will come to pass. I am asking for God's heart. I want what He wants. He will give me the desires of my heart as they are in line with His heart. I need this reminder every day. Let us not ask for what is not in God's will for our life or we ask amiss. That leads us to the next chapter, lead us not into temptation.

Key Takeaways:

- Operate from a healed heart, not scarred or broken.
- If we carry hurt around into our personal life, it will definitely show up at work too.
- Ask God to forgive us for our sins, and forgive others for what they have done to us.
- Pursue God's heart every day.
- Know the *right things* to ask and *have the faith* to really believe they will come to pass.
- God helps us produce good fruit (the fruit of the Spirt) in our life and business.
- We *cannot* produce these fruits sustainably or authentically over time without God's help.

Chapter Eight

Lead Us Not Into Temptation (Chasing Success, Money and Gurus)

Practical steps to sustainable success.

> *"This, then, is how you should pray: 'Our Father in heaven, hallowed be your name, your kingdom come, your will be done, on earth as it is in heaven. Give us today our daily bread. And forgive us our debts, as we also have forgiven our debtors. **And lead us not into temptation**, but deliver us from the evil one.'"* Matthew 6:9-13 NIV

How do we balance contentment versus striving?
Contentment is defined as a state of happiness and satisfaction. Striving is defined as a making great efforts to achieve or obtain something.

This is a really hard balance, especially as entrepreneurs. There are never enough hours in the day. We can always squeeze in one more appointment. We can always get one more client. We can always come in earlier the next day. We can always improve our website, our product, our service, top grade an employee, upgrade our office space, read another book, go to another seminar, get another coach, etc. It never stops! But the good news is that God made us that way. He built us to not just sit around and see what everyone else is doing, simply observing forever. If you are reading this book you are taking action to learn and become wiser. You are probably the kind of person I would like to get to know, because you are not settling for where you are today as being good enough.

God wants us to expand and take new territory for His Kingdom. He has given us the authority, the knowledge, the skills, the wisdom, and the encouragement to get up and get it done. There are a lot of religious people out there who would tell you it is a sin to be ambitious. Depending on your definition of the word, I can see how they might see it that way. If you are all about building *your* name and wealth despite what God wants for your life, then you could be heading down a dangerous path for your soul. Would you like a scripture to prove this?

"What good is it for someone to gain the whole world, and yet lose or forfeit their very self?" Mathew 9:25 NIV

"For where you have envy and selfish ambition, there you find disorder and every evil practice." James 3:16 NIV

Obviously, there is a balance between ambition/striving and contentment. What does the Bible have to say about the opposite way – contentment?

*"Keep your lives free from the love of money and
be content with what you have, because God has said,
'Never will I leave you; never will I forsake you.'"*
Hebrews 13:5 NIV

Since this verse brought up the topic of money, let me make a quick comment before I continue on about contentment. Ambition can become all about getting more money for some people, but notice what this does not say. The scripture does not tell us we cannot *have* money. The warning is to *not* fall in love with the money. Money will never love you back.

We should practice contentment with what we have, all the while knowing God can give us a big vision for the future. If we balance a healthy desire for wanting to advance God's Kingdom here on Earth with the satisfaction of what we already have, I believe we can achieve a proper mindset. Having a great mentor or business coach in this area would be really helpful. They can identify when you are sitting too idle and when you are pushing too hard, striving toward your God-designed destiny hastily or prematurely.

*"You are the salt of the earth. But if the salt loses its saltiness,
how can it be made salty again? It is no longer good for
anything, except to be thrown out and trampled
underfoot."* Matthew: 5:13

God wants us to be pure and to pursue our calling. He

wants us to remain steadfast in that pursuit! The reference to salt here has a couple of possible interpretations. My favorite is that He wants us to stay flavorful to Him and not lose our saltiness (considering all the contaminations of our world). We should have a different flavor than the world does. He wants us to stay focused on His Kingdom and His will for our life. He will put a unique desire on your heart or maybe even several unique desires and callings.

And by the way, it doesn't have to be a church-related calling like being a missionary in China or pastoring a church to be a real calling from God. He has inspired many small business owners and billionaires alike with great ideas and dreams. There are stories of scientists getting direct downloads, dreams and instructions for complicated recipes, formulas and unique uses for various things that would blow your mind.

Have you heard of George Washington Carver? He was a famous scientist who came up with over 100 uses for sweet potatoes and over 300 uses for peanuts. He wanted to give the world these uses to better the planet and the people. He has been reported to have been given these ideas by God Himself after long walks in nature. He became convinced of the existence of God through these scientific discoveries. "Never since have I been without this consciousness of the Creator speaking to me... The out of doors has been to me more and more a great cathedral in which God could be continuously spoken to and heard from."

I also believe that God doesn't want us to chase every business deal, business idea, new shiny object, exotic vacation, piece of jewelry, and anything else that becomes an idol to us to detract us from our purpose. Too many pursuits become distractions to our God-given calling and purpose. We need the Kingdom revelation of what God wants for us and what He doesn't want. We need to bring the Kingdom of God everywhere we go, including in our business and personal lives. God always wants to be with you!

> *God does not want us to chase every shiny object.*

So what does this have to do with temptation? If we are truly focused on what God's calling is for us (and we might have several callings), we should avoid temptation to pursue other things. I have several callings in my life. I am called to be Christian, an excellent husband, an excellent father, an excellent author, an excellent real estate business owner, an excellent friend, and an excellent business coach. Beyond that, other opportunities that may pop up are probably not for me or they may be for a different season in my future.

What are you called to do?
Take a minute and write down your callings in life and business. I will wait...

1.
2.
3.

4.

5.

This discussion is fun for some and painful for others. If it is fun, you may have more ideas than the margins of this book will hold. If you have some discomfort with this, you either have too many or too few callings coming to mind. Here are some questions that might help you find out if you are working your true field of favor or unique calling from God. Let me ask you some questions, and please write down your answers!

Where have you had victories in the past? Life, business, relationships, overcoming addictions, etc.?

Who do you love working with? What type of clients or customers?

Where do you like to work? Inside, outside, downtown, in the field, etc.?

Where do you have great experience, knowledge or expertise?

What hobbies do you enjoy outside of your day-to-day business?

What comes easy to you?

What networking/community groups are you already part

of or do you want to be part of?

Who do you aspire to be someday?

How do I seek godly wisdom for my business?

I believe we must align with Kingdom peers. It has been said that we are the average of the five people we spend the most amount of time with. Who is in your inner circle? What books are they reading? How do they spend their free time? What thought leaders do they follow? Are they part of a Bible-based church? Do they read the Bible? Do they pray? What does their marriage look like? Do they have a good family life? These are questions I would ask to make sure I am hanging around others on the path toward fulfillment in these areas of life.

"People who are going nowhere want you to go with them."
—Dr. Myles Munroe

You should also consider having at least one mentor in business and faith. This is someone who has achieved victories in areas you are hoping to gain territory in. I would recommend finding someone at church; someone a little older than you and ask them if you could have coffee sometime to chat. After learning more about each other, decide if you should ask them to meet once a month or whatever your time allows. This is one of the best strategies I have ever incorporated into my life.

I believe you should also have a good coach or coaches in

different areas. These are people you pay. I have had coaches in nutrition, fitness, business building, real estate, Kingdom entrepreneurship, and sports. Having someone who holds you accountable and looks at your life from the outside with a vested interest in your success is key to a better you in the future.

I highly recommend reading books and listening to podcasts. While driving around in my car I am always listening to sermons on podcast, stories from Kingdom entrepreneurs, Audible books and how-to's. I love to learn and continually renew my mind on these resources. In case you are interested in my favorite podcasts and books, I have included a list at the end of this book.

Finally, to seek godly wisdom I recommend going to seminars and meetups. There is something special about getting out of your comfort zone, maybe your city or state, and meeting with other Kingdom-minded entrepreneurs and business leaders. When sitting at your desk or on your couch listening to a webinar, online seminar or some YouTube videos, there is a propensity to cheat and do something else instead of pay attention. Deliberately changing your environment also lets us see things from a new perspective. I have met a ton of friends this way and stay in touch years later. Check out my favorite entrepreneurship conference on my Facebook page:

www.Facebook.com/kingdombusinesscoach

Key Takeaways:

- Contentment is defined as a state of happiness and satisfaction.

- Striving is defined as a making great efforts to achieve or obtain something.

- God wants us to expand and take new territory for His Kingdom.

- Ask your wise counsel if you are leaning toward striving for your own desires vs. God's Kingdom.

- God will put a unique desire on your heart or maybe even several unique desires and callings.

- Know what those callings are and prioritize them over other "good" things you can do.

- Read Kingdom books, listen to Kingdom Podcasts and attend Kingdom events.

Chapter Nine

Deliver Us from the Evil One (The Enemy Who is Trying to Stop the Kingdom of God's Expansion)

Keep the enemy away from your personal life and business.

"This, then, is how you should pray: 'Our Father in heaven, hallowed be your name, your kingdom come, your will be done, on earth as it is in heaven. Give us today our daily bread. And forgive us our debts, as we also have forgiven our debtors. And lead us not into temptation, **but deliver us from the evil one.***'"* Matthew 6:9-13 NIV

Who is the evil one?

Jesus called him "the enemy," "the evil one," "the prince of this world," "a liar," "the father of lies," and "a murderer." So it is safe to say that he is the bad guy in the story. People have been tempted since the fall (in the garden of Eden) by Satan. He has also tempted Jesus himself. Jesus said that He was tempted just as we are tempted. He overcame those temptations.

I have been tempted throughout my life in countless ways, just as you probably have. In my business, it is just as hard. I have also have been attacked by the enemy both in my personal and business life. The enemy wants to steal, kill and destroy. This includes wanting to disrupt and destroy our businesses that we have worked so hard to build and maintain. He also knows how much these businesses are part of our daily life.

I have had people come against me in my business in different ways. One time I had a client decide that she wanted to get a divorce with her husband. They were selling a home that I had listed for sale. Maybe she was embarrassed about the divorce or just didn't want to tell me the truth. She and her husband had moved out of this house months before she had made this decision, and now that she wanted to get a divorce, she wanted to stop the home-selling process and move back in with her kids. Instead of asking me to let them out of the listing contract we had all signed (which I would have gladly done), she decided to try and find faults with our marketing and sales process in order to get the contract cancelled. If she would have simply asked me to cancel the contract, I would have let her cancel it! Instead she went to our state board and claimed that I had not fulfilled marketing promises I had made in the listing presentation.

Although I knew these statements were not true and the accusations she made were not even violations of any kind of law, the state still had to do its due diligence and open up an investigation into me and my company anyway. It took about one year for them to investigate and then clear me from this mess. The whole time I kept telling my team that this situation was going to work out for good somehow. I remember quoting this verse:

"And we know that all things work together for good to them that love God, to them who are the called according to his purpose." Romans 8:28

This reminded me that usually these kinds of attacks are not personal. This lady did not really want to hurt me. The enemy is looking to find ways to hurt us and uses people to do the work. Paul told us that we are not fighting against each other, but against the enemy at work on those people to create strife and conflict. Here is what he wrote:

"For our struggle is not against flesh and blood, but against the rulers, against the authorities, against the powers of this dark world and against the spiritual forces of evil in the heavenly realms." Ephesians 6:12

How can we defend our home and business from the enemy?
Paul wrote some instructions in the New Testament for us as believers to equip and empower us for this battle:

"Put on the full armor of God, so that when the day of evil comes, you may be able to stand your ground, and after you have done everything, to stand." Ephesians 6:11 NIV

So we stand up to the enemy and put on the full armor of God. It is interesting that he tells us we do not need to actually fight. Why not? God promises us in the Bible that He will fight our battles. So let's focus on what to do to stand up to the evil one. What does that look like in our business life?

"Stand firm then, with the belt of truth buckled around your waist, with the breastplate of righteousness in place..."

In business this can mean several things. First, always speak the truth in everything you know. Second, seek the truth before making decisions. Third, I would recommend always telling the truth regarding the product or service you offer in your business. You do not want to omit important facts or exaggerate the offering you are making. Lastly, only use the truth when dealing with situations involving your clients, vendors and employees.

"...and with your feet fitted with the readiness that comes from the gospel of peace."

I have read many interpretations of this part of the scripture, and I believe God wants us to be ready to spread the message about Jesus at all times. We are to be ready to share our faith with our employees, clients or vendors as opportunities arise. So as we accept the peace Jesus offers, we should also be willing to share that peace with others at work and through how we conduct our business.

*"In addition to all this, take up the shield of faith, with which
you can extinguish all the flaming arrows of the evil one."*

The shield of faith at work is also vital. The first attack of
the enemy is usually doubt or fear. Sometimes it is a feeling
of distance because of sin. Jesus is as close to us now as we
can possibly comprehend so that is not the problem. The
problem is in our lack of faith about knowing He is always
near. And it is important we remember that He is as close
as our breath. We take up our shield of faith, so we can
stand strong against these feelings of fear, doubt or lack of
intimacy. Have faith that He is near you and will help you
overcome. Many times the enemy has tried to attack me
with feelings about not having enough money or clients in
my business. I have to go back to my faith in God, knowing
He will always provide for me in my business as I believe
I am in line with His will.

*"Take the helmet of salvation and the sword of the
Spirit, which is the word of God."*

This one is my favorites! I know that I am saved by the
power of Jesus. Being saved is more to me than going to
Heaven when I die. Salvation is complete healing in every
way. The Greek word "sozo" comes to mind as another
word for salvation. This can mean healing, restoration,
deliverance and making whole. I look at my business as a
gift God has given me. I am a steward of my business. I ask
God to save me as a person and help me build and
maintain my business well into the future. I ask God to

help my business stay healthy and whole. God does not want us to operate in brokenness or lack.

Is there hope for me, my family and my business?

There is hope for you, your family and your business. By putting on the full armor of God and with the Lord's Prayer as a guide, you can dive deeper into other scriptures throughout the Bible to help you in your pursuit of a successful life. When you are feeling anxious, afraid or nervous about an attack from the enemy remember to do these things:

1. Pray and ask God to help you with the situation and to fight your battle.
2. Pray for wisdom on what to do.
3. Talk to your spouse, friend, mentor or coach about the situation.
4. Read the Bible and ask God to show you key scriptures to help you.
5. Rest in God's goodness and mercy.

Key Takeaways:

- Keep the enemy away from our personal life and business.
- Keep in mind that we are not battling against each other, but against the enemy.
- Use the whole armor of God to stand firm against the enemy.
- Know that when you are saved, God is always close to you, no matter what you have done.
- Know that there is always hope for you and your business.

Chapter Ten

Summary

Okay, how am I going to keep all of this straight?

We've discussed so many things thus far, leaving you with a lot to think about. This isn't a book where you can read it in a couple of hours, get what you need and move on. I designed this book to be something you can refer back to over time when you need some help with one of these steps. From now on, each time you hear the Lord's Prayer spoken somewhere, my hope is that you think about the phrases just a little differently. Here it is one more time:

"This, then, is how you should pray: 'Our Father in heaven, hallowed be your name, your kingdom come, your will be done, on earth as it is in heaven. Give us today our daily bread. And forgive us our debts, as we also have forgiven our debtors. And lead us not into temptation, but deliver us from the evil one.'" Matthew 6:9-13 NIV

In summary, this prayer tells me we would be wise to:

Respect God and His Kingdom.
Do His will.
Do our best to instill His Kingdom here on Earth and in our

businesses.

Be content, but pursue the goals and dreams God has put in our hearts and minds.

Ask forgiveness for our wrongs and forgive others.

Remember to stay on course with plans God has given us and not be tempted to do someone else's plan or will.

Find wise peers, mentors and coaches and implement smart business techniques and strategies.

Let us do this all with love and humility. We are part of a big ecosystem, so we need to involve others in the process for sustainable success. We need to get to the place God has called us. Imagine a world where all of us walked out our divine purpose. Imagine the power of building a sustainable business or businesses that we can be blessed by and be a blessing to others through. Our churches, communities, schools and our nation need to be blessed by us! We need the fullness of God at work in our lives every day. When we walk into a room we bring the Kingdom with us! We need to be healthy and serve others to the best of our abilities, plus some!

"Whatever you do, work at it with all your heart, as working for the Lord, not for human masters." Colossians 3:23 NIV

Here is the point: we are designed to work. We are designed to work hard on things God gave us to do. We should work as if God is our client, whatever that looks like in your business. Stay motivated. Abide in God as your ultimate source of life and strength. Stay salty! The sooner we learn the systems God wants us to be a part of, the sooner we can become successful in our callings.

If you are wondering about God's systems, I have included some of my personal routines and systems as a suggestion in the Resources Section. Now remember, I am not a guru or a master of anything and cannot claim to have all the answers. I simply have some tools that have worked for me. Feel free to use these, modify them or use someone else's. The key is to create some kind of system to repeat your success; a system that works well for you.

Keep this truth deeply rooted in your heart: you are created in the image of God. We are His workmanship. We are created to be like God. He created us to be creative and find solutions to problems that other people do not see or do not have a passion to manage themselves. We are born to be leaders. People want to be led by strong leaders who inspire them. What are you doing to inspire others?

Over time, I have noticed that every single person has been through struggles and difficult things and has overcome them. In my life I have overcome some challenges and I seem to attract others who are going through some of those same challenges. Look back at your own past victories. Do you see any patterns? Are there at least a couple that have taught you some valuable life lessons? Well, guess what? These can be areas of life where your lessons learned can be helpful to others going through those same trials.

We are on this journey together. I recommend having strong friends; friends who will help you through good times and bad. During the good times they can keep you focused and humble. They can keep pushing you forward, not allowing you to get stagnant.

You will also have times when things are going poorly. Having great friends and mentors pushing you along and encouraging you is really key to coming out of the trial successfully and not getting stuck in it. We want to stay on the narrow path and not fall into life's alluring, short cut or fear-based temptations. These temptations will most certainly draw us away from God's will for our life. Think of a road trip you have taken to another state. It will require you to be on a highway for a long period of time. As you start off, you enter the highway from an entrance ramp and notice the cars around you. Some speed by, some are going too slow and others stay with you for a while on the journey.

For a period of time as your speed matches theirs, you see the same car or cars for maybe an hour or two. Eventually one of you has to exit the highway to get gas, take a bathroom break or move on to the next part of the journey on a secondary road. You should have relationships around you like that too. You are on the journey together with these people, traveling in the same direction and may get on and off the road together as you share some similar circumstances in your lives. These are important life seasons and are not to be ignored. In the same way, you can encourage other and be encouraged yourself when you are on the same road. Praying and seeking God and living a life of faith will help you stay on the right course, and rest assured God will put the right people alongside you during that part of your journey.

Keep in mind that entrepreneurs have a strong desire to *win*! We are *not* good losers. We never get used to losing. We also like to be on winning teams and pick other winners to come along with us on our journeys. If you look around to your left and right, who are you surrounding yourself with?

As entrepreneurs we also seldom follow others, unless that person has overcome challenges we see ahead for ourselves. We also tend to love problems, because we learn from them and solve them. We are problem solvers. Keep in mind that problems also precede miracles, so when we give God the driver's seat, sometimes these problems actually take care of themselves. So with God's help and our drive, we can usually get a lot done! We press on in spite of difficulties and we value opportunity more than security. We love to finish strong with excellence. Just do not let the spirit of excellence, which is from God, turn into a spirit of perfection. A spirit of perfection comes from our pride. We are never going to be perfect here on Earth. Let God make us whole.

I will leave you with these final power thoughts from various speakers at a recent 100X Academy Kingdom entrepreneurship conference I attended, which I believe summarize our mission as Kingdom entrepreneurs. I hope these motivate you like they did for me.

- Lead with love in everything.
- Make powerful decisions and take action on them.
- Remember that people everywhere are hungry for truth.
- Expand what you think is possible.
- Know your personal gifts and strengths.
- It is selfish to be poor on purpose.
- Listen to God more, talk less, daydream and think.
- You must go through a process before obtaining the promise.
- When you have an offer, have a guarantee and include it in your marketing.
- When creating an offer, give a free item of value.
- Have a compelling story and tell it!
- A great consultant will collapse time and money.
- Become an expert and earn authority.
- Accountability will accelerate results.
- Instead of setting big goals, set a big vision and plan.
- Catch the heart of the Father for your business.
- You are the average of the five people you spend the most amount of time with. Chickens become nuggets, eagles soar!
- Learn Kingdom principles and build your business from there.
- Money always follows value.
- Take steps of faith, even when you aren't 100% sure.
- Operate in your field of favor – everywhere else will be

frustrating, with little fruit.

- Look to your past where you have had victories and help others achieve those.

- Surround yourself with a supportive community with the same visions.

- When someone or something offends you, ask yourself why.

- You cannot have innovation without risk.

- Carve out a niche so tight that no one else can compete with you in it.

- Renew your mind daily with the Word and fresh mindset will come.

- Your vocation is your calling.

- We must steward our resources according to God's plan.

- This is a season in time like Joshua leading leaders into the Promised Land.

- You will never truly be ready to conquer your mountain; God will have to help.

- You get more anointing after winning battles, then go higher.

- Have a healed heart, a renewed mind, a Kingdom revelation, great marketing, a great offer, and operate in your field of favor.

- There are no shortcuts, but the Kingdom helps you achieve success faster and with less pain.

- The purpose of the cross is more than salvation, it is the wholeness of God.

- Don't ever lose connection with God – have unbroken fellowship.

- A prophesy reveals potential.

- God is looking for partners with great faith.
- All of God's promises are circling around waiting for someone to agree with them.
- Time management: it is either a fixed asset or God says it is redeemable (redeem time = to buy back, rescue).
- Time is a perception of reality, not *actual* reality.
- Get time back to its servant role, not mastering us. It is our friend.
- To bend time, begin in His presence, be teachable, have joy, abide, and protect your connection, have a purpose, and finish what you start in order to release authority.
- Create content from where you are now on your journey.
- Have Divinely-ordained partnerships.
- Be a garden hose – the inside is always wet from the blessings flowing through from the Source, through me, out to others.
- Abundance is found within your assignment.
- Seed involves giving *and* investing.
- Prosper in the work of your hand.
- God, You put Your blessing on me so people will know what You are like.
- Anxiety about money is worship of mammon.
- Faith is imagining your perfect future with God.
- Obedience is the greatest tool.
- I am the personal property of the King, along with everything I have.
- People are more important than money.
- Find good soil and sow as much as you can as fast as you can.
- Do not live offended.

- God has His mercy and grace on me.
- Paint a target on my heart that says GOOD SOIL.
- Avoid Kingdom landmines: the tug of war between ministry and business, being overly committed to the *how*, assuming all Christians are like me, wrong mentors, and going at it alone.
- Bring your thoughts into captivity.
- Have an infinite-possibilities mindset.
- Experience your emotions and deal with hurt directly.
- Stay connected to others who really love you and will be there for you.
- Mind changes matter.
- You are called to your world.
- Know who my WHO is.
- What problem does my WHO have that I can help them solve?
- What is the most expensive problem I can help solve for them?
- Build your own unique email list for free with a break-even offer.
- Do something that is impossible for you to do on your own. Have God-sized faith.
- Chase Jesus over profit.
- Be dependent on Jesus, having radical obedience to Him.
- Story braid during talks: speak to hearts, heads, hands, then heart again.
- Power of the story braid: people will never forget how you made them feel.
- The secret weapon for a great speech is the heart, the greatest marketing tool.

- Remember, when people go deeper, you have an opportunity to change their lives!
- Be vulnerable, willing to really connect with your audience.
- Teach, Teach, Teach, then Offer!
- There are many offers I can make after the speech to connect to my audience. An 80% capture rate is possible with a great offer.
- The highest calling in the Kingdom is to share, multiply, gain equity through sharing, leverage. Worst is economic slavery with assets and time.
- We don't have title (to our capital), we have responsibility and stewardship.
- Authenticity is paramount to success.
- The Kingdom is a weapon in business, displacing darkness.
- You have sonship, so run to your goals with boundaries/guardrails.
- Don't have an attitude of pride, but have a genuine concern for others.
- Be a peacemaker and inherit the Kingdom.
- Celebrate others!
- Death and life are in the tongue, our words matter.
- He is the CEO; I am the President.

Here are some affirmations you may want to speak out loud that I took from this conference:

I am covered with His love.

I have the mind of Christ.

I have a sound mind and think thoughts of love.

He has called me into this life.

He is with me always.

He is the Creator and will give me good plans for success.

He will light my path.

God will give me good seed to sow.

I want to be a leader raising other Kingdom leaders.

Now, your Kingdom entrepreneurship journey begins. Maybe you are starting from scratch. Maybe you are starting over. Maybe you have a renewed vision, purpose and energy. In any case, I pray this book helps you in some meaningful way along your own journey. Please email me or connect with me on Facebook or Instagram if you picked up anything specific from this book. It would be a huge encouragement for me.

In His love,
Derek

Key Takeaways:

In summary, the Lord's Prayer tells us to:

- Respect God and His Kingdom.
- Do His will.
- Do our best to instill His Kingdom here on Earth and in our businesses.
- Be content, but pursue the goals and dreams God has put in our hearts and minds.
- Ask forgiveness for our wrongs and forgive others.
- Remember to stay on course with plans God has given us and not be tempted to do someone else's plan or will.
- Find wise peers, mentors and coaches and implement smart business techniques and strategies.
- Resist the enemy with faith and putting on the whole armor of God every day.

Next Steps

Write down your key takeaways from each chapter in that section or in your journal. (See the Key Takeaways section at the end of each chapter.)

Pick out the next book to read and a class to take.

Explore getting a good business coach.

Ask to be added to a private Facebook group in your industry.

Recommend this book to a friend in business. Who do you know who would benefit from reading this?

Pray and ask God to reveal your true callings and purpose in life.

Join a small group Bible study.

Be a mentor and help encourage and develop the next generation of Kingdom entrepreneurs!

Resources and Routines:

Who God is to me:
I suggest looking up each of these scriptures and ask God to reveal Himself to you through reading them.

We have a King who is God (1 Timothy 6:15):
1. He is our Creator.
2. He is our Ruler/Master.
3. He has ultimate wisdom.
4. He has ultimate wealth and prosperity.
5. I am subject to Him; He owns it all.

God is the Word (John 1:1):
1. He is the Master of creation and has been there since the beginning of time, and even before!
2. He is living now.
3. He gives us revelation of Him through His Spirit-inspired Word (the Bible), spoken (via people) and given through prayer directly.
4. He is more complex than we can imagine and is able to work things together for our good.
5. He is beautiful and redeems our mistakes into a beautiful life.

God is the truth (Jeremiah 10:10):
1. He is the source of all good.
2. He is the light in the midst of darkness.

3. He is good despite all the evil around us.
4. He shows up different than we expect, like a baby born in a manger.
5. His truth is sometimes in contrast to what we think is true, but He is the source of all real truth.

God is the rewarder of my faith (Hebrews 11:6):
1. Jesus is the author of our faith.
2. Jesus is the finisher of our faith.
3. We are all given an equal measure of faith.
4. We must grow in our faith.
5. We have the opportunity and privilege of seeing things come true in our life; things we are believing for.

God desires our presence and intimacy (1 Cor. 8:3):
1. He is the source of all good, so we should want to know Him more. Get knowledge, understanding, then wisdom.
2. Companionship – He wants to walk through life with us.
3. He wants to call us Friend.
4. He wants to be our Abba Father, Daddy.
5. We can rest in Him and His goodness.

God is love and mercy (Ephesians 2:4):
1. Mercy is unlimited.
2. Mercy is undeserved.
3. Mercy from God is renewed every day.
4. Mercy is Jesus dying for our sins.
5. Mercy makes our best or worst efforts made better or redeemed.

We need God and have dependence on Him (Matt. 6:33):

1. He is the source of all good things.
2. He is the source of my business, not the resource for my business.
3. He knows and has everything we need.
4. He has our best interests in mind.
5. We were created and promoted to show His glory.

God is peace (John 14:27):

1. Jesus is described as the Prince of Peace.
2. The peace He gives us is beyond understanding.
3. We can grow daily in His peace.
4. Holy Spirt, our helper from God, will help us discover His peace.
5. Faith helps us to step into the rest He offers, the peace in our lives.

Jesus has all authority on Earth (Matthew 28:18):

1. We call on His name and use His name – we are His ambassadors.
2. We must claim the territory He won for us at the cross.
3. We must have confidence that He lives in us and we carry Him wherever we go.
4. We must boldly declare/speak: "I am His son/ daughter and have His authority."
5. We must stand on the promises of God in the Bible.

We are to be good stewards of God's resources (1 Peter 4:10):

1. He owns everything.

2. The parable of sower shows us to not hide the gifts, talents abilities, skills, money, etc., He entrusts with us.
3. There are two different systems to operate in on Earth: the world's system or His.
4. You must have a love for others like Jesus did. Love one another with what He has given you.
5. Don't focus on your possessions, influence, power or status. Focus on having a heart for God.

God gives us keys for our dominion of this world (Matthew 16:19):
1. Financial keys
2. Territory keys
3. Heart keys
4. Mind keys
5. Industries or "fields of favor" keys

We have joy through knowing Jesus (John 15:11):
1. Jesus is joy and our salvation! All who call upon His name and acknowledge that He is Lord will be saved.
2. Jesus gives us hope, imagination and dreams!
3. Love and joy go together.
4. Building the right relationships and community will result in more joy.
5. Jesus gives us a purpose that we are created for, and the fulfillment of that life brings us joy.

My daily routine (ish) on most workdays:
I fast breakfast completely, or mix a high-fat, no-carb coffee in my blender

Prayer

Gym time (with a Christian podcast or audio book playing)

Affirmations

Journal events of the past 24 hours (or catch up if it has been a few days)

Journal gratitude

30 minutes of email

2 hours of lead generation for my business

1 hour of lead follow up

Return calls from morning

Ketogenic Lunch (high fat, low carb, moderate protein)

Social media posts and content creation

Go on appointments

Negotiate any deals I have going

Dinner with the family around 6 p.m.

Spend time with my wife and kids (outside if possible)

Use the infrared sauna

Read 15 minutes before bed, usually by 11 p.m.

I recommend keeping your mind renewed daily. Learn something new!

Time block for daily reading

Prayer time for God's divine insights and downloads (hint: be quiet and listen)

Listen to great podcasts

Listen to great audio books

Read old-school printed books

Listen to online sermons, podcasts or YouTube videos

Attend a weekly small group Bible study

I recommend time blocking these things:
Quarterly and annual vacation
Daily tasks
Weekly tasks
Monthly tasks
Yearly tasks
Personal care
Business planning
Personal health (chiropractor, massage, acupuncture)
Fun activities
Serving opportunities

Here are some systems that I employ in my businesses:
CRM (customer relationship manager or database)
Email touch program
Client events to treat them to some fun (at least four per year)
Phone dialers for outbound calling efficiency
Coaching for myself
Scripts for me and all my employees

Choose your library carefully. What you read will help determine your future. Here are some books I would recommend:
Life in the Spirit Study Bible
Kingdom Principles: Dr. Myles Monroe
Every Good Endeavor, Timothy Keller
Sun Stand Still, Steven Furtick
Grace Revolution, Joseph Prince
Business Secrets from The Bible, Daniel Lapin

Thou Shall Prosper, Daniel Lapin
The One Thing, Gary Keller
Our Unfair Advantage, Dr Jim Harris
Pitch Anything, Oren Klaff
Start with Why, Simon Sinek
How Heaven Invades Your Finances, Jim Baker
Destiny, TD Jakes
The Finished Life, Pedro Adao
Grace Over Grind, Shae Bynes
The Ultimate Jim Rohn Library, Jim Rohn
The 4-Hour Workweek, Timothy Ferriss
Never Split the Difference, Chris Voss
The Alchemist, Paulo Coelho
Titan: The Life of John D Rockefeller, Ron Chernow

Podcasts I listen to:
100X
Church for Entrepreneurs
Kingdom Driven Entrepreneur
Believers Voice of Victory
TD Jakes
Elevation Church
Joel Osteen
Jesse Duplantis
Joseph Prince
Keto Lifestyle
Craig Groeschel
Creflo Dollar

Organizations I love:
100X Academy
Church for Entrepreneurs
At Work on Purpose
Kingdom Driven Entrepreneur

For the prayer I pray out loud each work morning before I start my day in the office, see page 69.

Affirmations I say out loud at the beginning of each work day:
We care about our clients more than selling.
We impact our clients' lives positively every day.
I am happy, healthy and it's going to be a great day!
We provide the best possible service available to our clients.
People love to work with us!
We love drumming up new business and take advantage of all possible networking opportunities.
I am a money magnet!
I do not take rejection personally.
I am confident when asking for business and referrals.
I provide value to my clients and those I wish to add to my fan club.
I speak positively about my business.
I will reach my goals only with God's blessing.
I always choose to do the right thing.
I am a Christian, a great husband, a great father, a great leader, and a great friend!
The future is bright!

I am becoming wealthier every day.

I am learning to master my time.

I choose faith over fear.

I will let the Holy Spirit guide me in what actions to take today and have peace about the results of what I get done through Him.

Mission statement I read aloud each work morning:

My personal mission is to build, inspire and love people so they live up to their God-given calling and live life to the fullest.

What is your mission?

_____

_____

_____

Goals I read out loud each work morning:

My Spiritual Goal is to become more like Jesus and make His name known to others.

My Relationship Goal is to build a stronger relationship with my wife and the kids.

My Business Goal is to get to $x per month in business income.

My Personal Financial Goal is to be debt free and all our monthly personal expenses paid by passive income and have at least six months of savings.

My Wellness Goal is to be healthy and strong till 120 years old.

My Travel Goals are to take a quarterly trip with Jessica

and at least one family vacation per year with the whole family.

If you have never accepted Jesus as your personal Savior and would like to, please say this prayer:

Dear Lord Jesus, I know that I am a sinner and I ask for Your forgiveness. I believe You died for my sins and rose from the dead. I turn from my sins and invite You to come into my heart and life. I want to trust and follow You as my Lord and Savior.

If you have prayed this prayer and would like a witness to this, please email me: **derek@derektye.com**. I would love to welcome you into the family of believers!

Thank you for reading this book. I pray that it is a blessing to you, your business and your spiritual walk with God.

—Derek Tye

Companion workbook available now at
www.kingdombusinessbreakthrough.com/workbook.

Testimonials

"It has been an absolute honor to work with you the past few years! You are a kind man with much integrity...and so knowledgeable about real estate! Here is to many more years of friendship! Blessings, with love and respect."
—Dede and Anthony Muñoz

"Derek shows up 100% every day in every way, I could not ask for a better overall person to be in business with!"
—Chrissy Ward, Chrissy Ward Team

"Derek is a truly altruistic and authentic man – giving in every aspect, an invaluable professional resource and wonderful person to know. As I was coming into the real estate world from another industry, knowledge, guidance and leadership were critical components for me to find. Derek, as one of our investors and top agents, provided this for me...and so much more! Whether you are looking for a partner on your God journey, looking for a coaching program, a podcast or a book to help you, you can count on Derek to serve you at a high level, deliver value and do it with a smile and caring heart. Enjoy the journey!"
—Jeff House, CEO KW 7Hills Realty

"I believe we meet certain people at times when we need them to open a door for our next path. After a few conversations over a listing Derek was selling, I quickly

knew he was a person I was connected to for a reason. Instantly relating to Derek's personal and professional values, I knew he was somebody I would like to work with on a consistent basis. Eighteen months later, my own business is thriving with the assistance of his coaching and mentorship. I'm grateful for that first 15-minute random phone call, as I'm now designing and living the life I want as a result of the relationship I've developed with him."
—Luke Luther, Keller Williams Realty

"I am going into my 25th year in the real estate industry and have had the privilege to work with Derek Tye for the last two of those years. As the Broker for the office, I see my fair share of agent-related issues and transactions. Not the case with Derek. His work and life are guided by his high standards, ethics and Christian background. He is an absolute pleasure to work with and an example for new and existing agents on how to run a business and live life to the fullest. Derek was instrumental in my decision to join Keller Williams Seven Hills. He took the time to meet with me personally, one-on-one, during my transition to answer some of my questions and assure me that he would be there to help me anyway possible. He makes the office a better place to work with his professionalism, his ethics and high levels of expectations."
—Chris Parchman, Principal Broker, KW7H

"Derek is an inspiration to the office. He has not only inspired me to be the best that I can be, he also brings this inspiration and encouragement to each and every person

he meets. Derek possesses an incredible knowledge of business and has even helped in the growth of my spirituality and health. No matter how big or small the problem may be, he is always there to lend a helping hand, never asking for anything in return."
—Rebecca Geiger, The Geiger Team

"Derek is an exceptional leader in the real estate field. He holds himself and those around him to the highest of standards, and that is evident in all aspects of his professional and personal life. He has a servant's heart for people and is unashamedly willing to help anyone who asks. I recently came to Derek to discuss how faith can positively intersect with my real estate career and he graciously gave his time and knowledge to me. I walked away from the conversation feeling much better about seeking extraordinary success so I could carry on what God has put in my heart for helping the less fortunate. I know I will come to Derek in the future for additional guidance. He is selfless in his approach to people. The other person's success is what Derek hopes to help them achieve."
—Jennifer McGillis, REALTOR®

"You are always open to helping a new agent, with a world of experience and knowledge, but most important is your heart and your sweet family. You have managed to keep centered on the humanity of what we do as real estate agents, and I am most sure that our Lord is well pleased." —Rose Manibusan, KW

"Derek and I have gotten into short, impactful conversations about my business. It has always started out as a small question that he turns into a coaching session, and I always feel like *man, I should've recorded that*! The nuggets of wisdom he hands out so charitably have been crucial in shaping my business this year. I can't thank Derek enough for all of his help with my business and life."
—Flor de Maria McNally, De Maria Team

"Where do I begin? I began working with Derek as an admin in his real estate business six years ago. During the multi-step interview process, the idea Derek wanted to make sure I understood was: "We do the right thing, the right way, and the money will come." As we worked side by side for several years, I witnessed all the ups and downs that come with real estate, along with some pretty intense mistreatment from clients and colleagues. This business can be incredibly competitive and many people operate with a scarcity mentality. Derek challenged his entire team from day one to work with an abundance mentality and to do the right thing for our clients and other agents, no matter what it costs. Our meetings always began with gratitude, and our team was (and is!) incredibly unique (for a sales team). I watched Derek lose money several times, by doing the right thing, but my respect for him only grew, as did that of our team members. And the ideas! Always a new idea, always a new business, always a "why not?" mentality. I joked with him all the time that he was "functionally insane" – that he was nuts, but functional! And, I witnessed firsthand over and over again how he poured himself into these businesses, with an expectation of success! And most of the time it worked! But even when it didn't, his attitude stayed positive and he learned what not to do next time. Working behind the scenes, I saw the numbers go up and down, I saw the deals fall apart, I saw the personal and professional tragedies, but I also saw the surprise deals that would come together just in the nick of time. I saw the friend of a friend who would give Derek just what he needed when he needed it. I saw that he did not allow his circumstances to determine his mindset, at least not for more than a few minutes. I learned so much working with Derek. In fact, I remember asking him once to teach me how to dream, how to set goals and accomplish them. And he was always willing to help, to coach, to listen and to give honest feedback. Sometimes too honest! But it's the only way that real change happens. I was privileged to work closely with Derek for a long time, and to hear the stories, personal and professional, the triumphs, the heartaches...and I have to say he is the most consistent person I have ever met. Not perfect by any stretch. He has ups and downs like anyone, but because he believes so strongly in his God, himself and his principles, he always comes back to center. And Jessy? She is the type of woman you want to dislike because she is so beautiful and accomplished, but you just can't! Together, the two of them have changed the lives of so many people they've come in contact with, through nutritional advice, real estate, success coaching, through their example of love and grace and always wanting more. They do not accept the status quo, but always want things to be better; better for their clients, themselves and those of us lucky enough to be in their sphere. They are two of the hardest working people I know as well and always stretching themselves, always learning and always giving. Even now I can text Jessy with a question about a supplement or a specific food and she will answer quickly. She doesn't have to – she's busier than any person I know, but she does it because she genuinely cares and loves to share knowledge. You know that quote by Hunter Thompson: "Life is not a journey to the grave with the intention of arriving safely in a well-preserved body, but rather to skid in broadside, thoroughly used up, totally worn out, and loudly proclaiming, 'Wow what a ride!' That's what I think of when I think of Derek and Jessy. They embody what it's like to live every moment, to optimize the gifts and talents you have been given, to genuinely care for those that society overlooks, and to point back to the Creator and show His love and creativity, living in gratitude and excellence."

—Claudia Hrinda, Re/max Team Administrator

"It has been my privilege to work for Derek Tye. I could quote the many accomplishments and accolades he has received, but the side that I like to bear witness to is his personal side. When often asked what the real estate mogul is "really like," my response is this. Derek, first and foremost is a man of God. He seeks God earnestly and applies His teachings to every aspect of his life. Derek is a devoted family man who adores his wife (and supports her business endeavors and personal interests as Christ loves His church) and takes great pride in teaching, loving and guiding each of his children. They are his pride and joy. Derek extends that same love and desire to guide and teach to his team of REALTORS®. He takes great joy in each member's accomplishments. Derek challenges and mentors his team in order for them to stretch and attain higher goals by setting a big vision. Derek always makes time for his team and others. He gives 100% of himself no matter what the mission involves. Derek is a natural-born leader and teacher. He knows what talents God has given him. He is obedient to our Father and knows what he is called to do and not to do. Derek loves being a REALTOR®. He is honest and forthcoming with his clients, even when the truth might be difficult for the client to hear. Derek cares for his clients and treats them as if they are part of his family, because in his mind, they are. Derek consistently delivers excellence and is a humble man who continues to grow in understanding by always reaching out to new mentors and praying for God's will in his life. It is my honor to work for and stand behind Derek as he formally moves into an "official teaching/mentoring role," which God has called him to. Without a doubt, those who have reason to come in contact with Derek are always blessed." —Lisa Cook, Greyline Technologies

About Derek Tye

"My personal mission is to build, inspire and love people to live up to their God-given calling and live life to the fullest." —Derek Tye

Author and speaker, Derek Tye, is an award-winning REALTOR® in the Cincinnati, Ohio, area. Along with his real estate work and investing, Derek's love of teaching and training others to reach their fullest potential has prompted him to create Kingdom Business Breakthrough Coaching, now with a podcast and classes.

Derek and his wife, Jessica, have five children, enjoy traveling, business, running their hobby farm, and living a healthy lifestyle.

Past-President and Director of the Southern Ohio Association of REALTORS®
1,300+ Homes Sold for over $300,000,000 in volume
2018 Top Sales Team/Group, Southern Ohio Association of REALTORS®

2018 Top Social Media Team in Cincinnati by
ThreeBestRated.com
Investor in a Keller Williams Realty Franchise
Realtor of the Year: Southern Ohio Association of
REALTORS® 2010
Real Estate Investor
Author
Speaker
Business Coach
Reach out today at **derek@derektye.com** or visit
www.DerekTye.com

Companion workbook available now at
www.kingdombusinessbreakthrough.com/workbook.

Hello brother or sister in Christ!

This is Derek Tye, and I am a Kingdom Entrepreneur. God has been working on me my entire life, developing my unique mission, value and purpose. I truly believe I have been specifically called to help Christian business owners get breakthrough in life and business and become Kingdom entrepreneurs.

I'd like to let you know about my podcast called Kingdom Business Breakthrough where I discuss concepts from this book in a live format. I also have invited several other Kingdom Entrepreneurs and thought leaders on the podcast to help spread the good news. Join us on the podcast!

Lastly, would you like a copy of my free guide to Holy Spirit Led Business Planning? Get this free guide instantly by visiting:

www.KingdomBusinessBreakthrough.com
Simply fill out the form with your name and email address!

In Him,
Derek Tye
www.DerekTye.com
Facebook: www.facebook.com/kingdombusinesscoach
Instagram: @KingdomBusinessCoach

Speaking

Looking for a dynamic, compassionate speaker for your organization's next event or meeting? Contact Derek Tye today for more information on having him speak for your business association, small group, church, leadership team, marketplace ministry group and event, podcast, conference, webinar, men's retreat, and more.

Derek can tailor speaking topics for your group or event on themes such as:

- Vision and Life Purpose
- Kingdom Entrepreneurship
- Intersecting Circles in Your Field of Favor

To book Derek to speak at your next business, real estate or faith-based event, contact him at
derek@derektye.com.

Exclusive Publishing for Kingdom Entrepreneurs
www.100Xacademy.com